Frontispiece
Wrought iron and brass brace supports a console table in the Royal Sitting Room.

Title page
The living room furniture includes an Italianate damask quilted sofa, a coffee table of walnut burl inlaid with brick parquetry pattern on open trestle supports, trapunto-quilted circular swivel hostess stools with round canted legs, green lacquered side tables with Canton famille rose vases mounted as table lamps, and ledge-back chairs with wavy brick-motif stitching.

Text, design, and all archive images
© The Annenberg Foundation Trust
at Sunnylands 2023.

Images have been provided in many cases by the owners or custodians of the work. Individual works of art appearing herein may be protected by copyright in the United States of America or elsewhere, and may not be reproduced in any form without the permission of the rights holders. In reproducing the images contained in this publication, The Annenberg Foundation Trust at Sunnylands obtained the permission of the rights holders whenever possible. In some instances, the Trust was unable to locate a rights holder, notwithstanding good-faith efforts. The Trust requests that any contact information concerning such rights holders be forwarded so that they may be contacted for future editions.

All images and photographs are from the Sunnylands Collection, with photographers credited and page numbers noted.

Contemporary photographs illustrating this catalog are by David Loftus, taken in December 2022.

Official White House Photographs:
6–7, 26 (left), 132.

All rights reserved by Peter Schifando and William Haines Designs: 14, 28, 34, 38, 46, 50, 58, 60, 68, 78, 82, 96, 100, 104, 106, 109, 116, 118, 122, 130, 136, 145.

Photo by Julius Shulman © J. Paul Getty Trust. Getty Research Institute, Los Angeles (2004.R.10): 16, 36.

Photo by Russell MacMasters: 18.

Photo and drawings by A. Quincy Jones and Frederick E. Emmons Associates: 34, 38, 44, 116.

Drawing by Harry W. Saunders: 84.

Published in 2023 by
The Annenberg Foundation Trust at Sunnylands,
37977 Bob Hope Drive, Rancho Mirage, CA 92270,
United States of America.

All rights reserved. No part of this book may be reproduced or utilized, in any form or by any means, electronic or mechanical, without prior permission in writing from the publisher.

Library of Congress Control Number: 2023901657
ISBN: 978-0-9913420-8-2
Printed in China

Editor: Ashley Santana
Book and Cover Design: JCRR Design

This page

Canton famille rose vase mounted as a lamp shares the table with a late-Qing Dynasty cloisonné enamel crane.

Opposite

Ivory-painted, bamboo-style open armchair with lemon-yellow quilted fabric.

Contents

Foreword by David J. Lane — page 6
William Haines Design: An Expert's View — pages 8 – 11
The Designers — pages 12 – **21**
The Dream Team — pages 22 – 31
Desert Regency — pages 32 – 39
The Tent — pages 40 – 69
Beyond the Tent — pages 70 – 85
Outside the Main House — pages 86 – 101
Design Signatures — pages 102 – 139
A Design Legacy Preserved — pages 140 – 145
Endnotes — page 145
Acknowledgments — page 147

Foreword

Each year, a novel Sunnylands story is unveiled in the gallery at Sunnylands Center & Gardens. With each exhibition comes a deeper exploration into one of the many subjects that intersect with Sunnylands. Whether it be design, diplomacy, art, or the natural history of this storied estate, each topic is curated into an educational exhibit. The exhibition research is also published as a catalog such as this, creating a canon for the Sunnylands heritage site.

This year, the focus is the interior and furniture designs at Sunnylands. William Haines, a legendary designer, brought his vision for an extraordinary design to Leonore and Walter H. Annenberg. Visitors to the Sunnylands estate today, whether on a public tour or as a participant in one of our retreat programs, often remark that Sunnylands provides a special and elevated experience that can in part be attributed to the unique setting and design.

From the impressive archives that the Annenbergs carefully retained and assembled at Sunnylands, we have a wealth of information about the estate. We know the Annenbergs intended for their desert home to be a place for family, friends, and colleagues to spend time together. The public spaces extend beyond residential scale, suggesting that large gatherings were prioritized in the original design. However, we see no evidence that the Annenbergs anticipated and planned for what happened next.

Both Leonore and Walter would be appointed as ambassadors representing the United States within 15 years of the first guest book signatures at Sunnylands. These new roles expanded their national and international social circles. Political and other leaders across various disciplines became regular visitors, resulting in Sunnylands becoming a place with significant convening authority.

The Annenbergs observed over the years that the special experience at Sunnylands, with its thoughtful design promoting connection and conversation, contributed to the forging of relationships. Following the Annenbergs' wishes, it is precisely the unique experience of gathering with others at Sunnylands that the Trust continues to provide today, thereby advancing impactful conversations and outcomes for the greater good.

Ambassador David J. Lane (retired)
President, The Annenberg Foundation Trust at Sunnylands

Opposite

In conversation: U.S. President Barack Obama and His Majesty King Abdullah II of Jordan, with delegation members, in dining room during a dinner meeting at Sunnylands on February 14, 2014. A Brazilian rosewood round dining table with ivory inlaid circles, stained walnut dining chairs with hand-painted brown tortoiseshell-pattern leather, on canted legs, and Chinese-style, pale-green-painted side cabinet with Georg Jensen silver candelabra, circa 1935, and pale green jadeite figure of a recumbent water buffalo, Qing Dynasty. Hanging on the celadon green wall is a replica of Claude Monet's painting *The Stroller (Suzanne Hoschedé)*, 1887.

WILLIAM HAINES DESIGN: AN EXPERT'S VIEW

Patrick Dragonette, an interior designer and a dealer of 20th-century furniture specializing in Haines, shares his insights.

Q: When you first saw Sunnylands, and you comprehended what had been done there, what was your impression? How does the Sunnylands Haines collection compare to others, past and present?

A: I was very privileged to experience Sunnylands for the first time with Jean Mathison, who had run the offices at William Haines, Inc., for 30 years. She was the only person still living who had been involved with the design. I had seen pictures of the main room many times and so I was excited to see it in person. What I didn't expect was the overwhelming emotion that came over me; it moved me to tears. I have said many times that Sunnylands must be experienced in person; no photo can convey the majesty of the space. My initial thought was how amazing that this will be here and cared for so that everyone can experience this magical place.

I think it is worth noting that in spite of the fact that the main room is quite large because of the floor plan, it doesn't seem overwhelming. Haines understood how a space should be used, and this is a perfect example of that. The seating groups create intimate "rooms" within the space. His repetition of furnishings creates a calm that from a less-talented designer might have been the opposite. His use of symmetry also contributes to the calm. There is no doubt in my mind that all these choices were intentional and made for the reasons I have stated. I have not yet addressed the amazing finishes that are used throughout the property—again, something that creates calm.

Unfortunately, this is, to my knowledge, the only intact Haines interior still in existence, so it has no competition! I have been privileged to have viewed several Haines interiors prior to their being taken apart and carted off to auction, and each one has been as unique as its owner. The real beauty in Sunnylands is that it is open to the public and will always remain intact. Much of what Haines created has been scattered to the four winds. I have sold many of his pieces to collectors in Australia, France, and England. There are not enough pieces in museums, and now many of them have left the country.

Q: Why is Haines considered a design master? What characterizes or typifies Haines? How should we understand him?

A: Haines earns the title "design master" because his work was unique and singular at a time in history when the midcentury esthetic was everywhere and "modern" was the style of the moment. Haines realized that without the past there can be no future. To honor the past in many of his designs and yet to make them something new and different was one of his great gifts. In designing interiors, he would always include antiques, many times in fresh ways. His use of important Chinese ceramics and other objects to fashion armature lamps is a prime example. Wanting to include these beautiful things and yet preferring to keep clutter to a minimum are typical instances of this.

In characterizing Haines, in my experience, his eye for style was equal to his need for comfort. I have never seen a Haines chair or sofa that wasn't as comfortable as it was stylish. His understanding of proportion and comfort served him well, as did his understanding of living well. He expressed that in his designs. He was a social creature who hosted black-tie dinners, like many of his clients, and so he understood what made a house gracious to company. Portable seating was a signature, in the form of small chairs and stools that could move with the conversation. What good is a chair that isn't comfortable? His case goods [unupholstered furniture] are also an example of his modern style, always pitch perfect for where they were intended.

I would say that a signature characteristic in Haines' work would be the way he could take very simple forms and embellish them through special fabric treatments, of which there are stunning examples at Sunnylands. Look no further than the upholstery. Consider the simple forms the seating takes, and then notice the detail in the embellishments—quilting, crewelwork, trapunto, and leather finishes. And as for the case goods, many Haines pieces feature a special paint finish, perhaps only used for a specific project. Looking around Sunnylands, one can see the unique finishes that were used.

Lastly, I think it is important to point out that Haines, unlike many of his contemporaries, never designed anything for a commercial manufacturer, available to the general public. Everything he designed was made only for the project for which it was intended, and therefore the work is finite. Having a living museum like Sunnylands is a gift to us all.

Previous pages

Detail of folded corner treatment on red leather-wrapped game table with stained walnut legs amidst yellow bamboo-style open armchairs with leather seats in the Game Room. Playing cards and other games was a core Annenberg family pastime. Hence, six custom game tables were integrated into the original furniture plan.

Q: What is it about Sunnylands that is typical of the Haines and Graber design? What are the pieces that you think a visitor should focus on because they really do express the genius of these two designers?

A: The simple answer is *everything*. When designing a home, the clients were always at the forefront of a design. How would they use the house? Would they entertain? What were their pastimes? Were they collectors of fine art? All the answers were "yes," and are present in Sunnylands when you think about it. The house is an entertainer's dream. The backdrops created for the art are subtle and let the art do the talking. The game tables and chairs in the Atrium show that games played an important role in time spent at Sunnylands. No detail is overlooked in this interior. Walter required a proper office, and his is a stunner. Leonore loved a dinner party, hence the addition of the large dining room a couple of years into their using the house. The fact that the property continued to change is proof that a house is a living thing and can continually be guided by an experienced eye.

I think that, for me, the true standouts and a real signature are the lamps. There are so many examples of armature lamps where beautiful antiquities were lovingly mounted as table lamps without compromising the integrity of the item. The pair of water buffalo lamps, with the Lucite armatures in the hall outside of the Room of Memories, have always been favorites of mine. I am not aware of another designer who created lamps as singular as these. Also, in that hallway, the pair of eagle-form side tables are unique—most likely the only ones ever made. In terms of classic Haines, the chairs around the table near the west window in the living room are signature chairs and are not to be missed. It is hard for me to discount any of the designs since they are all important, and to see them all relate to one another is magic.

Q: Why are Haines furniture pieces and lamps collected and integrated in residences today?

A: I think the easy answer is because they are beautiful. For some collectors and designers, it is a chance to own something with a history. I know that for me part of the allure is wondering who sat on that chair before you, who dined at that table? Most of Haines' clients were very social and extremely well connected, so their guest lists were the ones we all might have envied. Knowing that the pieces have had a rich history can be irresistible for some folks. Since there is not a lot of this furniture on the market, the rarity is also a draw. And finally, let's not forget the fact that they are some of the most beautiful designs ever. Who wouldn't want to surround themselves with beauty!

Q: What else would you want to share about Haines designs?

A: I think in a period of design when so many designers seemed uninterested in the past, Haines came along and embraced the past and breathed new life into it. His designs pay homage to the past but are also very modern. There are people who refer to the Haines esthetic as "Soft Modern," and it's a term I think he would have liked. As a designer, I have learned so much from this modern master, and I will continue to study his legacy. As a man, he forged a new path as well, refusing to conform to a Hollywood system that demanded he remain in the closet. Haines lived an honest life with his life-partner, Jimmie Shields, until his death. It was this authenticity that led him to his second career as a decorator—and we are all the better for it.

Left

Patrick Dragonette standing in the living room next to a *gemütlich* [cozy] table with Brentwood chairs in painted frames and upholstered in gray leather, green lacquered side table, and damask drapery.

THE DESIGNERS

The Interior Designers: William Haines and Ted Graber

The interior design world is replete with amazing and artistic people with unique talents as well as flair for creating inspired spaces. An iconic home designed by extremely gifted decorators can fashion the ultimate in interior design as well as connect the residence with a homeowner's vision and lifestyle. This is undoubtedly the case at Sunnylands, the impressive jewel known as the Annenberg estate in the Sonoran Desert, with interiors and furniture designed by William Haines. His original designs for wealthy and well-connected clients established a high-level statement of distinctiveness and an enduring style that is instantly recognizable today.

Mayer Rus, a design editor, defines the Haines style thus:

> *Trademarks of his work from that period included one-of-a-kind lamps fashioned from exotic artifacts; hand-painted Chinese wallpaper and other accents of chinoiserie; and custom furnishings that riffed on historical models. His penchant for reinterpreting antique forms by giving them sleeker, more tailored silhouettes—in particular those of classic English and French Regency furniture—helped spawn the term Hollywood Regency, a style that cycled back into vogue for entertainment industry pashas and design aficionados in the early 2000s.*[1]

Opposite, clockwise from top left

Detail of Walter Annenberg's kneehole office desk with gold tooling embellishments on brown tortoiseshell-pattern leather with brass handles on rosewood drawers. The contiguous gold detail is rolled on and corner emblems are stamped.

Detail of a console hallway table with wood pierced brackets, raised on round tapered legs with partially ring-turned capitals and bases in the Steuben hallway.

A textured, low, upholstered elbow chair with ebonized flared legs was once positioned near the coffee table in Walter's office for drop-in guests.

One of twenty dining room chairs with hand-painted brown tortoiseshell-pattern leather with gold tooling embellishments and tapered paneled backrest, on canted legs. The labor-intensive process included painting the tortoiseshell design on the leather before upholstering the chair, then touching up the leather as needed.

Previous pages

Green lacquered end table resembling the stone malachite, with Chinese ceramics and biscuit-tufted armchair, on pink-hued and black-bordered marble tile floor.

Right

Colored rendering of dining room chairs in gold-tooled, brown tortoiseshell-pattern leather with front, side, and back elevation. The differences between these watercolors and the final built chair illustrate the iterative design process that ultimately resulted in a more upright and squared-off backrest design.

Charles William "Billy" Haines (1900–1973), actor-turned-tastemaker decorator and furniture designer, is known for his Hollywood Regency design style. Haines combines sleek custom-made furniture with interiors that mix period English and French antiques, Asian objects, and modern aesthetics. Haines came to Hollywood in 1922 after winning a "New Faces" talent contest and appeared in over 20 films as a silent-screen romantic leading man to famous women movie stars. Haines was a popular box office draw and during this period opened an antique shop in 1930 with former roommate Mitchell Foster on La Brea Avenue in Hollywood. The next year, they formed the partnership Haines Foster Inc. Haines acting career ended in 1934 due to his refusal to deny his same-sex attraction. He left the movie industry to reinvent himself as an innovative, self-taught decorator and designer. Haines' early celebrity clients included Hollywood luminaries, like his first client, Joan Crawford, in 1929, as well as Gloria Swanson, Carole Lombard, Jack L. and Ann Warner, and George Cukor.

Foster retired in 1945, and Haines renamed the firm William Haines, Inc., and in 1949 relocated his business to 446 South Canon Drive in Beverly Hills. The new building, Haines Studio and Offices, was designed by architect William F. Cody FAIA (1916–1978) in collaboration with Haines himself. The prominent architectural photographer Julius Shulman (1910–2009) shot photographs of Haines inside his studio. What is interesting to note is that Shulman assigned the photoshoot project number 446, the same street number as the Haines Studio and Offices, a curious numbering coincidence.

Opposite, clockwise from top left

Haines and Graber integrated lamps directly into furnishings, as seen in this example that merges a yellow lamp into a faux-verdigris glass-topped table in the Yellow Room.

Haines designed Lucite boxes in a variety of shapes with a netsuke fastened on the lids for each guest room. The Annenbergs filled them with room-colored jellybeans, a tradition the Trust continues today.

Caning and wickerwork are elements Graber brought to his work at Sunnylands, as seen in this wicker-veneered cabinet (detail) designed circa 1974.

Haines ignored no table edge, as evidenced by these gold tooling embellishments on red leather-wrapped and walnut library table, one of a pair.

Right

Haines Studio and Offices included cork walls for pinning drawings and brass pulls for draping textiles. Haines shows fabric to Barbara Lennox, a *Los Angeles Times* reporter. Black-and-white photograph by Julius Shulman, 1949.

Ted Graber (1920–2000), son of a cabinetmaker and antiquarian, joined Haines in 1945. Graber was a professionally trained designer and furniture maker, and became a young associate and protégé of Haines. "Their association lasted for nearly three decades, with Haines often attributing much of his success to Graber."[2] After Haines passed away in 1973, Graber continued the business with significant commissions, including iterative changes within Sunnylands as well as creating the interiors for the later-added guest building. He also designed the White House private quarters for President Ronald Reagan and his wife, Nancy. Graber stated about this highly visible project: "I've always said that I do a job only if it's fun…and this is no exception—it's a pleasure."[3]

Designer Peter Schifando joined Graber in 1986, and when Graber retired in 1989, he sold the firm to Schifando to continue the William Haines, Inc. legacy by offering authentic reissue custom-ordered furniture based on original Haines designs. Vintage custom-made furniture and furnishings by Haines are highly coveted by dealers, collectors, homeowners, and interior designers around the world. Original custom Haines pieces can be found in the secondary marketplace, including design studios, galleries, shops, and auction houses.

Opposite

Details of a nine-foot-long, altar-motif table, one of a pair, in the Royal Sitting Room. Trestle supports are joined by wrought-iron braces and a horizontal stretcher.

Below

Ted Graber seen here at his Brentwood residence, circa 1980–1981, worked with Haines and the Annenbergs on the interiors of Sunnylands as well as the complete refurbishment of Winfield House, the official residence of the United States Ambassador to the United Kingdom. Graber retired in 1989.

In His Own Words

A selection of Haines' candid comments on design appeared in *Architectural Digest*.[4]

Opposite

One of five color-coded guest rooms, the Pink Room features a glazed writing table with canted corners on tapered legs accompanied by a quilted bamboo-style open armchair and a quilted sofa in a "scattered roses" motif cotton fabric.

Design is an opinion, not a profession.

Who is to say what is good taste and what is bad? I don't know what taste is. It's like a fog … you can see it and feel it, but you can never touch it.

I contend there's no decorator in the world who can make a house good if the architecture is bad.

A house is a shell. The people who live in that house make it come alive and no designer in the world can do that for them. They have to make it their home. They must possess the house; it should not possess them.

You can buy anything in the world if you want to pay for it. You tell me what you want and I'll get it for you.

The Dream Team and Sunnylands

The American media magnate Walter H. Annenberg (1908–2002) and his wife Leonore (1918–2009) were fine-art collectors, philanthropists, patrons, and American Ambassadors. They resided near Philadelphia and were actively involved in social and political circles. In 1966, they built their winter residence, Sunnylands, in Rancho Mirage, California.

The stately beauty of Sunnylands was a direct result of collaboration between the design team and clients. This involved the architects and designers who planned the buildings and interiors, landscapes with gardens and lakes, and a private nine-hole golf course. This team, with constant input from the Annenbergs, was able to successfully turn 200 acres of raw desert scrub into a green desert oasis. In 1972, Haines describes his forward-thinking approach and viewpoints on the value of a collaborative composition for a successful project design team:

> *The interior decorator, the landscape gardener, and the architect should all be consulted in the beginning. They should work together before they present anything to the client. As it is now, a client buys the property, hires the architect, [and] brings in an interior decorator. Then when the house is almost built the landscape architect is called in. That whole process is completely backwards. The three should be hired as a unit and work together. Each one should know what the other is doing. Also, the architect should respect the decorator as much as the decorator respects the architect. That's the way we work, although it does not mean everybody should work that way. I am only speaking about William Haines, Inc., and that has been our philosophy for years and years.*[5]

Previous pages

A painted garden bench, evoking a whimsical insect with angled legs, supports a green marble top.

Above right

Letter and photograph from William Haines regarding a mosaic floor design, April 16, 1965.

Right

Dream Team—Leonore Annenberg (center), William Haines (behind her right), Ted Graber (her immediate left), A. Quincy Jones (behind Graber), Sunnylands site, circa 1963.

Opposite

Chaise lounges with pierced circular frames, in a suite of green metal outdoor furniture, adorn a mosaic "rug" on the south patio, creating an inviting outdoor living space.

The architect A. Quincy Jones FAIA (1913–1979), in collaboration with Haines from 1948 to 1951, designed the renowned Frances and Sidney Brody Residence in the Holmby Hills area of Los Angeles. The Brodys were friends with the Annenbergs and their home captivated Leonore. She wanted to engage the same team to build and design their desert property into a majestic residence of their dreams with harmonious atmosphere, elegance, and modern sophistication. In April 1963, Haines introduced Jones, a professor and later dean at the School of Architecture at the University of Southern California, to the Annenbergs. This initial meeting was the launch of their successful working relationship with the Annenbergs. To build Sunnylands, the architectural team of Jones and partner Frederick E. Emmons FAIA (1907–1999) collaborated closely with the designers Haines and Graber, who specified the interior floors, wall finishes, lighting, and furnishings. The early plans for the Sunnylands landscape were the influential work of landscape architects Emmet Wemple (1920–1996) and Robert Herrick Carter (1919–1989), and were further developed by landscape architect and horticulturist Rolla J. Wilhite (1924–2014), along with internationally renowned golf course architect Louis Sibbett "Dick" Wilson (1904–1965).

Opposite

One of a pair of wrought iron and brass marble-top consoles installed on a mirror, doubling the depth perception. Ming Dynasty–era hare-form roof tiles were slyly paired by Walter Annenberg with Picasso's *Au Lapin Agile (At the Nimble Rabbit)*, 1905, connecting the two rabbit narratives. The original painting is now at the Metropolitan Museum of Art (Met) in New York City; a replica is in its place at Sunnylands for historical context.
A painting reproduction in the background, whose original is also now at the Met: *Antoine Dominique Sauveur Aubert* (born 1817), *the Artist's Uncle, as a Monk (Portrait of Uncle Dominique as a Monk)*, 1866, by Paul Cézanne.

Above

President William J. Clinton and Walter Annenberg in 1995, admiring Pablo Picasso's 1905 original painting *Au Lapin Agile (At the Nimble Rabbit)*.

Right

Dream Team—Walter Annenberg (center), A. Quincy Jones (far left), William Haines (with necklace), Sunnylands site, circa 1963.

The Haines correspondence files at Sunnylands document serious discussions as well as the decision-making process on design details, furniture selections, fabric choices, item inventories, and important project topics. The friendly banter between Annenberg and Haines about food and assorted missives is highly amusing and lively:

Dear Bill:

Your December 11, 1964, communication regarding the cottages and the furnishings thereof has a labyrinthine quality to it. You are quite right—I am more confused than ever.

Sincerely,

Walter[6]

A 1965 letter illustrates Haines' sense of humor:

Dear Walter:

Thank you for the 'Ford Times' with its delicious recipes. Yes, I agree, the crab and chicken Cordon Bleu sounds just great!

I have one complaint left with the Almighty; he gave us two of almost everything for pleasure but a stomach which now has become important at my age. The other single pleasures have escaped into oblivion and even now, the memories are dim. But a full belly is something that one can feel and rub with joy and contentment.

Wouldn't it be nice to have two—one for the stuffed crab and the other for the chicken Cordon Bleu?

As Ever,

Bill[7]

Right

Drawing of *Gemütlich* [cozy] *Table* with iron supports and pedestal base detail. William Haines, Inc., Design #1704, 1964. Cozy tables were a staple in Haines' designs.

Opposite

Gemütlich [cozy] table in walnut with ivory-inlay and a hexagonal top, iron C-scrolled supports, and pedestal base surrounded by light gray leather Brentwood chairs with painted frames. *Gemütlich* tables were intended to inspire conversation and game playing in social settings. The wrought iron detail of the table support is echoed in the graduated tier supports on the chandelier overhead.

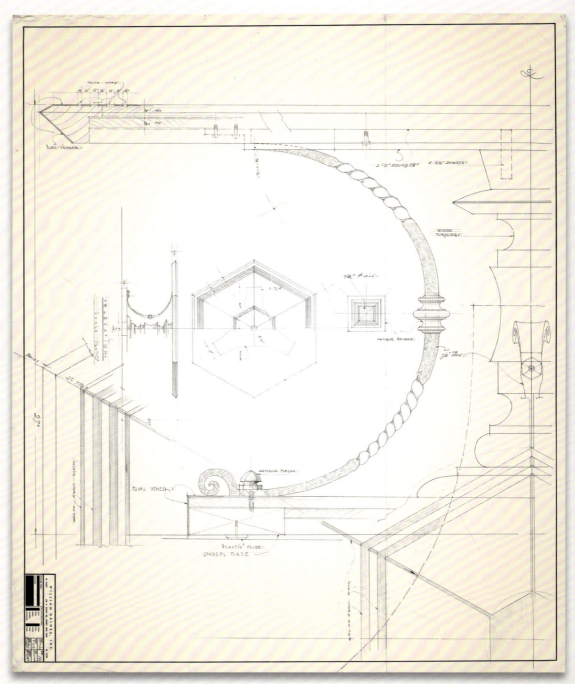

It took three years to complete Sunnylands, with the first entries appearing in the guest book on March 8, 1966.

Some two weeks later, on March 21, A. Quincy Jones wrote:

"Everything good—heaven" and a year later, on March 23, 1967, Haines and Graber inscribed:

Haines—"It was almost worth it!" and

Graber—"It was wonderful doing it"[8]

Opposite

Brazilian rosewood dining table with ivory-inlaid circles and bands and a Sunnylands guest book displaying William Haines and Ted Graber inscriptions dated March 23, 1967.

Below

From left to right: Jimmie Shields, Ted Graber, William Haines, and Walter Annenberg in front of a private aircraft, circa 1967–1969.

DATE	NAME	RESIDENCE
5-23-67	William Hines	It was almost worth it!
3/23/67	Ed Palee	It was wonderful doing it
3/24/67	Joseph R. Neff	
3/07/67	Sidney Weinberg	The Eighth Wonder of the World has been created!
28/67	Daphne Liss MacIntosh	Wonderful —
/67	Red to Hélène Motley	It's beyond description
	Margaret Willard	Home was never like this!!!
	Peter S. Paine	
	Sis Lea Paine	We LIKE!
	Pamela Churchill Hayward	Me too
	Leland Hayward	
	Adeline Seemann	
	Mimi Gross	
	Sylva Buchan	April 15

DESERT REGENCY

Hollywood Regency Rejects Desert Modern

The revolutionary audacity of Sunnylands' architecture and interiors cannot be fully appreciated in the 21st century. One must harken back to 1963 when Walter and Leonore Annenberg stepped—no, leapt—into a project that was not without design risk. In an era and a region heavily leaning into a minimalist, modernist interior design, the Annenbergs, Haines, and Graber embraced a full-on maximalist approach.

After the Annenbergs secured 200 acres on the former Wonder Palms Road in now-Rancho Mirage, the designers erected a massive steel tent in the sand, which is today recognized as an iconic structure known for its pink pyramidal roof. When the Annenbergs came to the table with their vision for an extraordinary desert home, they not only asserted their arrival in the desert but also cemented their permanent place in the international architectural conversation. Sunnylands' soaring architecture might have intimidated most designers, but Haines delivered them their ideal. Leonore once said: "I love it…if you were to close your eyes and build your dream house, it would be your dream house."[9]

Haines avoided predictable clichés in his canon of work, and the Sunnylands project is no exception. There is scant evidence of then-popular postwar materials that were informing popular interiors at that time. Bent plywood, dark walnut wood paneling, references to the space age, and fiberglass would have been too trendy for Haines' approach to design. His design vocabulary was well established, and he brought this confidence to the Sunnylands interiors, despite the narrative suggested by acres of sand and a pyramidal-shaped roof.

Previous pages

An iconic Haines tableau pairing Chinese antiques with his own modern version of a Chinese table. Cloisonné enamels, from left to right: Qing Dynasty vase, Middle to late-Qing Dynasty shrine, Ming Dynasty incense burner, and below, a large Qing Dynasty lidded jar. A Middle to late-Qing Dynasty cloisonné enamel crane candleholder stands in front of the fireplace, one of a pair.

Opposite

Qing Dynasty, rare, cloisonné enamel table, one of a pair, with Ming Dynasty blue glazed elephant armature table lamp and living room furniture. These tables were the only antique furniture installed at Sunnylands by Haines.

Below

Rendering illustrates Sunnylands' pyramidal roof and section through the house, showing courtyard, bedroom, and main living area with furnishings, as well as silhouettes of people. A. Quincy Jones and Frederick E. Emmons sheet, 1964. Though a fireplace is drawn, it appears that a chimney had not yet been designed for the roof.

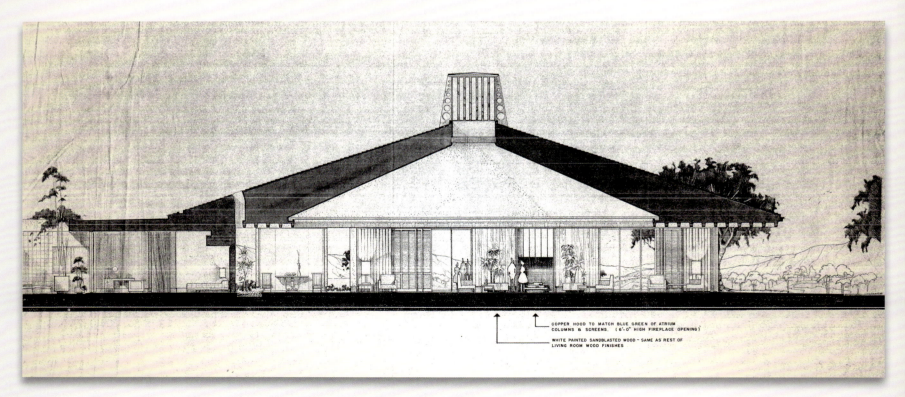

Teaming up with the Annenbergs in the Sonoran dunes, Haines had decades of experience with narrative estates. One project of many, which can be seen as a precedent for Sunnylands, was the Beverly Hills home he had designed in 1937 for Jack L. Warner, co-founder of Warner Brothers Pictures. *Architectural Digest* was still talking about this home in 1992:

"With its 13,600-square-foot Georgian-style mansion, expansive terraces and gardens, two guesthouses, nursery and three hothouses, tennis court, swimming pool, nine-hole golf course and motor court complete with its own service garage and gas pumps, the nine-acre property was—and still is—the archetypal studio mogul's estate."[10]

The article went on to say that the house achieved convening authority at the time:

"Few homes, moreover, compared with the Warner estate as a social milieu in the thirties and forties."[11]

Haines repeated this success at Sunnylands in that it, too, became a center for American political and societal gatherings in the seventies and eighties and continues that legacy today as a retreat location for important meetings.

Opposite

This 10-foot version of Haines' iconic ledge-back sofa on heavy runner legs is paired with matching "Seniah" ("Haines" spelled backward) chairs in the Game Room. The ledge-back design is an iconic shape in the Haines canon, dating to 1947. The room features hand-printed sunflower bouquet quilted fabric in a wavy brick pattern, executed in nubby linen.

Below

The Annenbergs, inspired by the Frances and Sidney Brody House, commissioned the same design team for Sunnylands, their winter residence. Haines designed the Brodys' living room, recorded in this color photograph by Julius Shulman, 1952.

The Sunnylands main house, comprising 25,000 square feet, can be thought of as two distinct spaces. The first is a dramatic Atrium entrance revealing a soaring, 20-foot tent space given its pyramidal-shaped roof. The additional areas in the home are accessed by two hallways, which lead off the tent in opposite directions.

Opposite

Haines' pairing of antique objects with stylish, custom furniture is a repeated motif throughout the house, lending a sense of continuity to each space. A late 19th-century jade boulder carved in low relief lends gravitas to the scene set on an eight-foot, stained-oak credenza, one of a pair, with canted edges and shelved interior. A pull-up chair, with trapunto seat, stands by for enlistment as additional seating.

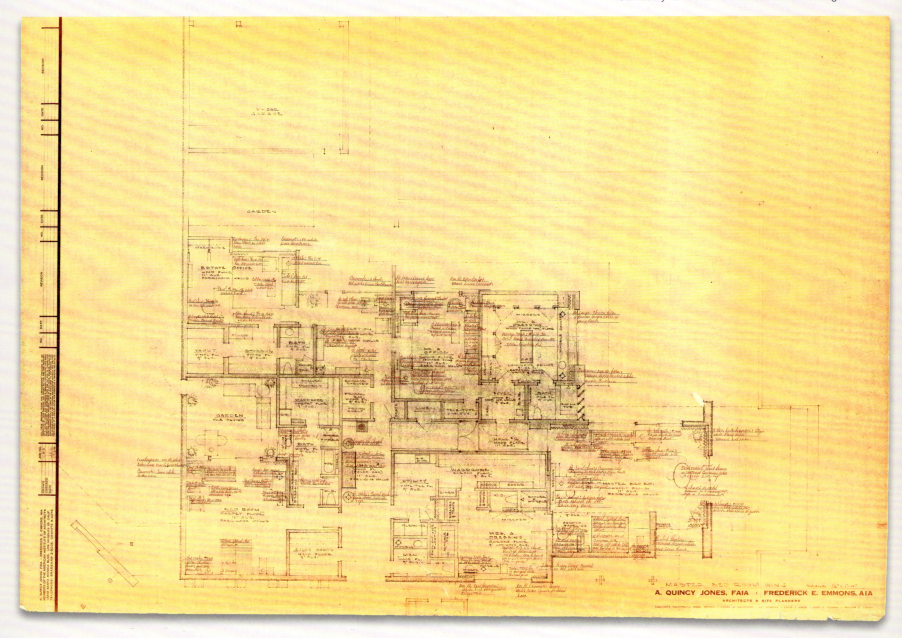

Above

Haines' notations for furnishings were overlaid in red pencil on an A. Quincy Jones architectural drawing. Plan of the *Master Bedroom Wing*. A. Quincy Jones and Frederick E. Emmons, Project #246 sheet, 1964.

A 12-foot, ledge-back sofa treated in quilted damask anchors this conversation area with two open armchairs on canted legs. The four tables share a cast iron, faux-verdigris finish, but the variation to the theme is found in the tabletops.

THE TENT

The Annenbergs' art collection of Impressionist and Post-Impressionist paintings hangs on the lava rock wall. These are full-scale digital reproductions within carved duplicates of the original ornate picture frames.

Wide-angle view of living room furniture. The Annenbergs and Haines shared a love for pairs and symmetry, illustrated here in the heart of the house with mirrored suites of furniture echoing mirrored architectural elements.

Walter and Leonore brought to the design table a vision to create a modern iteration of Mayan Revival architecture in the desert. In 1963, Walter wrote to the senior associate editor of *National Geographic* magazine:

"I am contemplating the construction and development of a home in the desert area of southern California and am planning this project in terms of the Mayan influence. I have taken the liberty of suggesting to my decorator, Mr. William Haines, of Beverly Hills, California, that he might communicate with your office to see is it possible to secure reprints of any editorial material that would reflect the Mayan civilization and its influence."[12]

References to their vision were delivered through the built structure rather than décor—specifically, the pyramidal-shaped roof inspired by Mesoamerican pyramids. Mexican lava stone tiles clad the indoor-outdoor walls running 30 feet in one direction and 32 feet in the other, framing the front door entrance along two axes. Pink-hued marble tile floors cover the entire expanse, while a trickling, dark-green marble fountain under a central skylight is filled with tropical plants. The skylight is reminiscent of an Aztec temple roof comb (crown). On the motor court a 20-foot-tall Mexican bronze column is carved with the narrative of ancient Mexico. These references to the civilizations of Central America begin and end in the architecture.

Opposite

Black marble borders within pink-hued marble tile help define spaces and alignment of furniture. Haines was active in designing integrated structural elements, including wall and floor treatments.

Below

Architect A. Quincy Jones delivered the Annenbergs a bold, architectural masterpiece with a pyramid-shaped roof punctuated by a pierced, vertical skylight structure likely inspired by the architecture of roof combs—structures that top pyramids in monumental Mesoamerican buildings.

If architectural design follows intent, the tent was created for entertaining at the highest possible cinematic level. Haines entered this unusual space and made it his own. He designed the interiors as well as nearly all the furniture. That said, the Annenbergs held a strong voice on this project. Ideas flowed freely among Haines, Jones, and the Annenbergs. For instance, Walter inquired in a letter to Haines whether he would be straying from his established vocabulary and would introduce elements from modern Mexico. Specifically, Walter had admired narrative frescos while visiting that country and wondered if these might be considered. Haines replied with his typical wit balanced with deep knowledge. He responded that he did *not* want the décor to simulate an American Mexican restaurant—which is where Americans might have seen Mexican narrative frescos in the 1960s. Explicit expression on a Mesoamerican or Mexican theme within the interior design was therefore avoided; and Haines' team was of course prescient to do so. With one misplaced cultural reference, things could have gone wrong very quickly.

Opposite

Four exposed cruciform columns suspending a signature A. Quincy Jones coffered, dropped ceiling define a center garden and fountain. Haines designed variations on a theme for each side of the garden, segregating various usages including a game area. Heavy oak credenzas are placed to anchor and create a square, more-intimate living space within a large rectangle.

Left and below

Colored renderings of two side-table designs. Similar tiered tables were fabricated for Sunnylands with a variety of finishes.

Conversely, during the give-and-take of design conversations, Walter and Leonore prevailed in rejecting an exaggerated elevation for the house, which might have suggested too explicit a reverential or sacred tone as true pyramids are designed to convey. Walter later wrote: "I finally convinced the architect to bring the house down to ground level instead of having it elevated 12 feet. He had in mind some sort of pyramid effect."[13]

These design conversations provide evidence that the Annenbergs and Haines were not interested in developing a literal Mesoamerican-themed estate despite having a bold pyramid in their roof choice. The roof shape also did not influence architect Jones to remain on any particular theme. He managed to introduce his signature "egg-crate," coffered ceiling design under the tent—a device he had utilized in his own home in 1939 and many times since.

Opposite

Haines' design influence is seen in the use of lightly sandblasted and green-painted redwood wall paneling along with the choice of pink marble floors, seen in this view of Royal Sitting Room furniture. Above the sofa is a replica of Claude Monet's painting, *The Path Through the Irises*, 1914–17.

Below

Haines' triumph is demonstrated in beautifully scaled furnishings within a complex architectural framework, as seen here in the living room.

Furniture Plan in the Tent

The interior design of the tent provides a master class in controlling and humanizing a large space through scaling—that is, bifurcating the space into groupings of furnishings and the employment of subtle variations on a central theme creating overall cohesion.

Since the tent area is approximately 5,850 square feet, Haines wrestled the massive space into smaller "living room" spaces. The marble fountain beneath the skylight divides the space into three different gathering areas known as the living room, Atrium, and Royal Sitting Room (a space used as the dining room pre-1974). Standing atop a marble turntable plinth in the center of the fountain is one of August Rodin's masterpieces, *Eve*, a life-size figurative bronze. The turntable rotates to face *Eve* into any of the three gathering areas in the expanse. Over the years, however, she has remained facing the front door.

Opposite

The welcoming interior design, set within soaring architecture, is complemented by the faint scent of tropical bromeliad plants and the sound of trickling water from the fountain featuring the bronze sculpture's plinth. *Eve*, 1881, an artist's proof by Auguste Rodin, was acquired specifically for this location.

Below

This colored rendering of a console table with marble top demonstrates that Haines envisioned each piece of furniture within the context of surrounding wall and floor treatments. This table, one of a pair, was executed exactly as drawn.

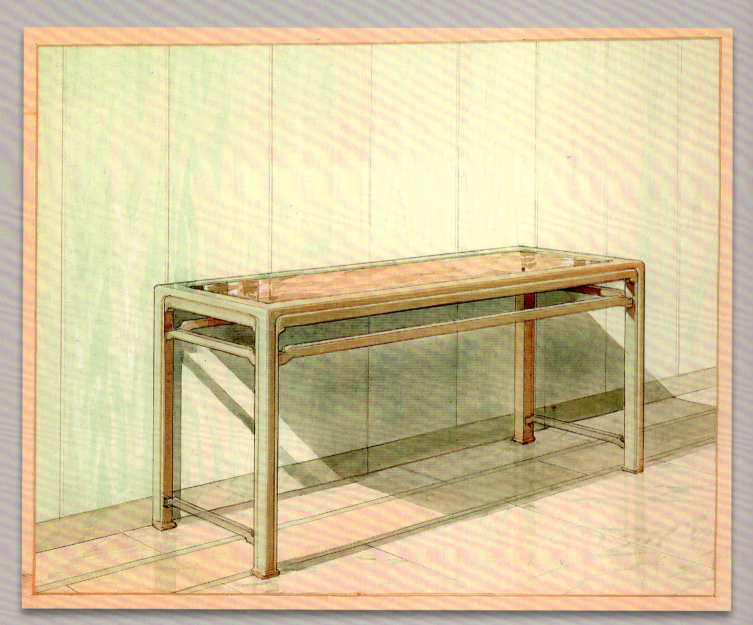

Haines further segmented these three spaces into inviting clusters of furniture, lighting, and accessories. Overall, there are six sofa-anchored "living room" setups to choose from to sink into for a conversation, cocktails, and hors d'oeuvres. Each setup utilizes a variation of Haines' classic conversation arrangements with various combinations of pull-up chairs, "Seniah" chairs ("Haines" spelled backward), and/or trapunto-quilted hostess stools on canted legs positioned opposite the sofa to achieve intimate conversation zones.

In addition to the sofa setups, there are spaces designed for games, as the Annenbergs were avid players: one custom backgammon table in the Royal Sitting Room and two square game tables in the Atrium. Another space for gathering is a six-person, *gemütlich* [cozy] table, with a complex geometric inlay, anchored by a soaring wrought iron, brass, and gold leaf chandelier on the west side of the living room. Adjacent to this space are two additional clusters of soft furnishings on which to perch, anchored by biscuit-tufted armchairs and turquoise-glazed tables. Designing the space as clusters of furnishings within the expanse, Haines created a variety of chic areas in which to gather underneath the canopy.

Opposite
Game table with leather upholstered chairs on turned legs in the Atrium. The Annenbergs were avid card players, mainly bridge. Hence, two game tables occupied a permanent place in that room.

Above
Button-tufted chair in slubby silk blend fabric with celadon canted legs.

Once the space was segmented into lovely islands at which to socialize, the further genius of the design is found in the subtle variety of furnishings, treatments, upholstery, and tabletop artworks. Yet colors, textures, and scale remain in concert throughout. For instance, the 50-plus upholstered pieces of furniture in the Atrium and living room share just two different fabrics, and remarkably, mostly just one: a sumptuously, gently textured, celadon-hued slubby silk blend is the ground fabric for all but eight of the soft furnishings. A custom Italianate floral damask in tan and celadon green is used as an accompaniment. The celadon-covered furniture displays a variety of treatments: biscuit-tufting appears on one group, trapunto diamond-shaped quilted relief or floral medallions adorns other pieces, and six of the larger trapunto-quilted pieces enjoy an additional overlay of hand-embroidered flowers in crewelwork. It is the variety of treatments on the same ground fabric that creates an illusion that a variety of coordinated fabrics are in play.

Opposite

In a Haines interior design, chairs are stationed to maximize social interactions. This pull-up chair was installed at an angle, allowing leg room. The seat is treated to an intricate design in trapunto quilted relief. A Chinese-style coffee table features an antique hardstone-mounted lacquer panel, flanked by black lacquer fretwork panels, one of a pair.

Right

Chair with diamond-shaped, trapunto-quilted fabric with overlay of blue-and-white crewelwork embroidered flowers. The winding flowers introduce nature inside the house.

This variation on a theme approach applies to the ten tables in the Atrium as well. A vertical spindled frieze decorates the underside of all ten tables in the vast Atrium. Yet the table materials and finishes are disparate. The tabletops are alternately marble, thick Lucite, or leather with gold tooling. They all share the same distinct structure but with entirely different treatments. This discipline to cohesion with subtle variations is Haines' forte.

Opposite

Surrounded by furnishings covered in a custom, Italianate, floral damask, all the tables in the Atrium feature the same design under the tabletop, though they are treated to a variety of tabletop materials and base treatments. This faux-verdigris table base supports a thick canted marble top, one of four. The sofa, reminiscent of a chaise, is one of a pair.

Right

A Mexican, silver, duck-form box, with jeweled eyes (one of a pair by TANE Mexico) stands sentry facing the front door from its perch on a leather-wrapped game table with spindle-frieze design.

Leather upholstered wooden chairs, rather than luxurious stuffed furniture, are employed when activity-based sitting is required in the tent as well as elsewhere in the house. They are replaced at the game tables and at the *gemütlich* [cozy] table when sitting upright is necessitated. Extra leather chairs and silk-covered benches line the walls so they can be pulled toward the sofa-anchored clusters for additional guests. Haines furniture is at once luxurious, comfortable, and inviting, rather than stiff and precious. The individual pieces, in lovely arrangements, set the stage for an elevated experience in the space.

Opposite

One of eight, this leather Conference Chair is an iteration of a classic 1949 version Haines used in his designs. Featuring a curved walnut paneled back with pierced top rail and wings, the turquoise leather, inverted D-shaped seat on flared legs is a showstopper. Haines originally called this design "Dining Room Chair" but a later-designed dining room altered the use of these chairs in the house.

Below

Drawing of *Front Elevation of Dining Table Chair*. William Haines, Inc., Design #1699, circa 1964–1965.

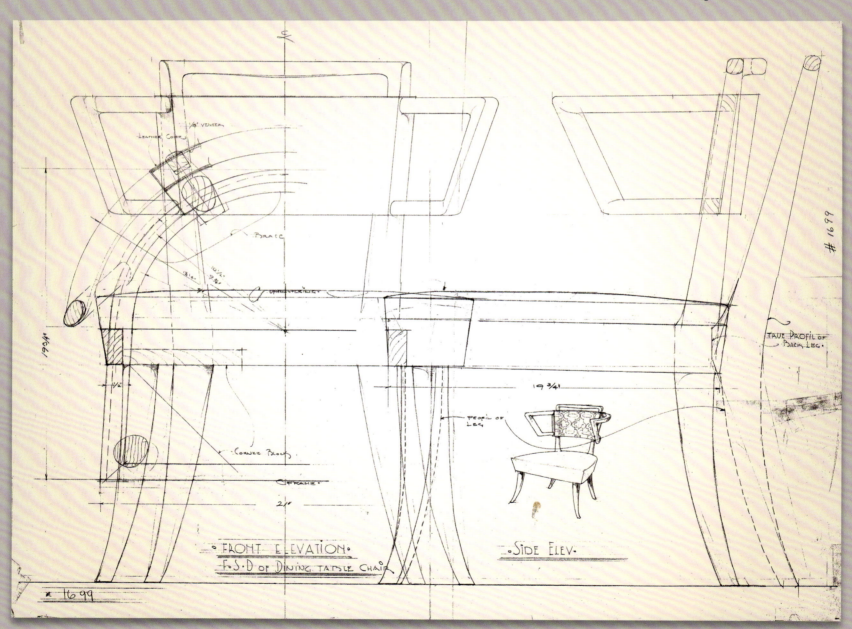

Hollywood Regency: The Details

As mentioned earlier, over the span of Haines' career, of which Sunnylands was arguably the highlight, his work has become synonymous with a style called Hollywood Regency. This moniker was called out, given his (and others' at the time, circa 1930s) use of furniture that references the furniture popular during the English Regency period inclusive of the later reign of the Prince Regent: 1811–1830. Design is eternally iterative, so it's important to note that Regency furnishings themselves were a revival of classical motifs from antiquity, namely ancient Greece, Rome, Egypt, and others. Thus, in essence, Haines designed furniture that references classical silhouettes. In his early work in Hollywood, antique furniture and accessories dating to the Regency period and earlier were interspersed with his own newly designed furniture that referenced antique furniture. Other elements of the Regency period style were pulled into his earlier designs, such as the use of fanciful fabrics and patterns. In fact, textiles were used in abundance during the Regency era, with swaths draping walls and hung from ceilings emulating a tent-effect. Faux finishes and applications of inset details such as metal were brought into Haines' designs, emulating the Regency predilection. Regency draperies were voluminous with heavy tassels. Antique tabletop accessories were Chinese or Egyptian. Chaise lounges were immensely popular, an ancient Egyptian influence. Interiors during the Regency era hit a high mark. The overall look and feel is that of a magical, classical fantasy—and Haines brought this into his body of work.

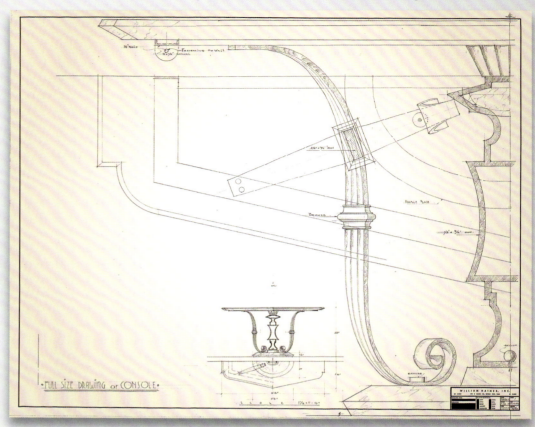

Opposite

Console with marble top and iron supports, with sculpture *Chapeau-forêt (Forest Hat)*, 1960, by Jean Arp, below a replica of *Camille Monet dans le Jardin Argenteuil (Camille Monet on a Garden Bench)*, 1873, by Claude Monet, and Atrium furniture in background.

Above

Drawing of *Console* with iron support detail. William Haines, Inc., Design #1696, 1964.

Left

Console table with cloisonné enamels: a Qing Dynasty vase (left) and a Ming Dynasty incense burner (right).

At Sunnylands, however, working with the midcentury master A. Quincy Jones, Haines left the antique furniture behind and designed nearly every piece of furniture himself. Instead of Regency-era side tables or antique Chinese altar-style tables, punctuated by carved Chippendale mirrors, Haines designed streamlined, modern versions of Regency-inspired furniture. Antiques were limited to tabletop curiosities and for lamps, a look he was known for and that he pulled into this design. At Sunnylands, modern, abstract sculpture also dots the interior landscape and interplays with Ming-era roof tiles in a successful mashup of periods.

Examples include two chaise lounges installed in the Atrium as one enters through the front door of Sunnylands. These reference classical Egyptian furniture, albeit they are built on modern runner legs rather than classical feet. They are structured with a muscular modernity instead of being curled. Flared legs are used for numerous chairs at Sunnylands, a direct nod to a classical Klismos chair, yet are modernized via exuberant faux-turquoise-inspired leather. Oxbow stretchers, inlaid Chinese hardstones, molded legs, and fretwork appear on and in Haines' Chinese-style coffee tables, altar-like tables, and cabinets. Heavy, modern walnut cabinets anchor the living room alongside rare Chinese cloisonné end tables dating to the Kangxi Period (1662–1722): a triumphant juxtaposition and the only antique furniture in the furniture plan. Deep, upholstered chairs are covered in a wavy brick-quilted pattern and swivel on inset, bulky modern turntables.

Opposite

Hostess chair with curved backrest, geometric trapunto-quilted seat, and canted legs. Sunnylands has more trapunto-quilted treatments on furniture than any of Haines' other projects throughout his career.

Below

Conference chair in stained walnut with curved wings and turquoise leather seat detail.

View across the living room. Architect A. Quincy Jones created a perfect playground for Haines to execute his mastery of scale, color, and warmth within grandeur. The interplay of angles and textures, heights and dimensions, remains timeless. Jones designed a coffered dropped ceiling and extended it outside to provide shading for the patio areas as well as adding a visual architectural element to the roof eaves.

The fireplace is starkly modern, a flat plane with no mantle, yet it is flanked by tall, Chinese, crane-form candleholders that once graced a Chinese palace. This surprising juxtaposition provides a perfect example of Hollywood Regency design. At Sunnylands, draperies are tasseled, but subtly. Haines further expanded the explicit interpretation of Regency with modern lines on the sofa arms and backs and placed them on iconic Haines runner legs. Though modern, the soft furnishings are all covered in the most luxurious fabrics available, a balancing of the two vocabularies.

For Haines, as was true of Regency furniture, all chair and table legs and every tabletop provide an opportunity to add layers of over-the-top detail for additional interest. Sunnylands' wood furnishings are thickly glazed in boisterous colors or inlaid with geometric patterns. Tables are treated to canted edges with ring-turned supports. Glazed motifs for tabletops include brick, faux malachite, and faux tortoiseshell. Numerous pairs of colorful Chinese antiques-turned-lamps mounted on modern supports punctuate the spaces, a dramatic note for which Haines is well known.

Above

Haines was a master at many things, including finding charming pairs of antique Chinese objects for use as lamps. These Qing Dynasty turquoise-glazed female and male Foo dog (or lion) table lamps sit on what Haines called "museum mounts."

Opposite

A brick parquetry pattern coffee table parallels a floral damask sofa and trapunto-quilted circular swivel hostess stools. A clear priority for Haines was ensuring enough seating. Hostess stools (foreground) were peppered around low tables, creating a warm invitation to additional guests who might pop in on a conversation.

Haines reflected his love and respect for the Regency period in such furnishings as Chippendale-style mirrors, silk wallpapers, draperies with oversized tassels, gilded antique English sconces, and heavy chandeliers dripping with crystals for the Annenbergs' Philadelphia-area classic colonial home, which he later decorated. Luckily, today, in the dining room and the sitting room off the primary bedroom called the Inwood Room, one can see the mashup of Sunnylands modern (architecture as well as décor) with authentic Regency-period English furnishings and accessories that migrated west to Sunnylands when the Philadelphia home was sold in 2007.

Opposite

Chinese-style, pale-green-painted dining room side cabinet on runner legs with Georg Jensen silver candelabra, circa 1935, and a Chinese export circular porcelain box, circa 1785. This functional cabinet provides storage for an extensive linen collection.

Below

Colored rendering of Chinese-style dining room side cabinet on runner legs with painting above. This painting remains paired with this cabinet today.

BEYOND THE TENT

Variations of Grandeur

The wings that extend off the central tent lead to the primary bedroom, his-and-hers offices, a kitchen, a dining room, a den known as the Room of Memories, and a since-removed indoor pool now-convening space. Additional areas include the former staff bedrooms and other back-of-house spaces, such as an industrial laundry room that once housed its own ironing machine for feeding in and crisping bedding and linens. These volumes scale down on a gradient as doors off the tall and wide hallways lead into cozier spaces with lower ceilings.

Previous pages
A spectacular walnut television cabinet with inset latticework over a painted ground to match the upholstery in the Room of Memories is flanked by leather upholstered mahogany open armchairs with tapered and flared rear legs. A portrait of George Washington by Rembrandt Peale, 1859, overlooks the scene in this intimate den.

Below
Detail: Haines never missed an opportunity for additional details, illustrated here by the gently curved, upholstered backrest and the ebonized bands of stained mahogany on this armchair.

Opposite
Haines' bold color choices are on display in the Room of Memories. This stained, walnut library table, one of a pair, is wrapped in bold red leather with gold tooling embellishments and trestle supports. A nesting table is seen below. *Portrait of Walter Annenberg*, 1978, by a friend and neighbor in Philadelphia Andrew Wyeth observes the scene.

The interiors for these ancillary volumes are more familiar in scale. Haines delivered his magic touch in all of them, such as his-and-her swivel-top nightstands that rotate over the bed. Haines cleverly changes the mood of each space by activating the same devices that he enlisted in the tent.

Opposite

Swing-arm bedside table with drawers, painted faux-wood grain paneling, and famille rose porcelain vase integrated as a table lamp.

Below

Biscuit-tufted upholstered bench in yellow and white floral damask. Deep button tufting requires fabrics that can successfully stretch.

First, the luxury level for the entire house is elevated throughout, yet each space rings a slightly different tone in terms of fabrics, wall treatments, accessories, and lighting. Most important to Haines' technique is that in each of the spaces all the pieces work harmoniously together on the micro-theme of that specific room, and all align to a specific level of luxury. For instance, the Chinese cloisonné objects on the side tables in the formal tent are largely imperial-pedigreed, and most date to a specific era of the Qing Dynasty, his and the Annenbergs' favorite: the Qianlong reign (1735–1796). The pair of cloisonné lamps in the cozier den, while still museum-worthy examples of the art, are of a different quality from the 19th century.

Opposite

A coral trapunto-quilted sofa in a diamond design with matching "Seniah" ("Haines" spelled backward) swivel chair. Upholstered circular hostess stools in a raised relief waffle-pattern fabric, glass and walnut coffee table, and late-Qing Dynasty cloisonné enamel table lamps. The memorabilia remain exactly as the Annenbergs placed them in the Room of Memories.

Right

Detail: one of a pair of late-Qing Dynasty cloisonné enamel vases mounted as lamps. The colors and iconography of Qing Dynasty-era cloisonne were of particular collecting interest to Haines, as opposed to the Ming Dynasty-era when blue enamels were more navy blue in tone and less vibrant.

Secondly, the interiors are color-coded. The primary bedroom palette is yellow, the Room of Memories boasts a coral-color motif, and the dining room is grounded in celadon green, which is painted on the redwood paneled walls as it is in the tent.

Left

Colored rendering of round table. This table was executed in two sizes as imagined in this watercolor painting.

Opposite

Set dining table with turned legs and gold tooling embellishments on brown tortoiseshell-pattern leather chairs. Round dining tables were preferred by the Annenbergs, who avoided hierarchical, "head-of-table" seating.

Below

Drawing of *Living Room Round Table* (later installed in the dining room) with inlaid ivory bands and circles on tabletop and supported by rosewood-turned legs. Williams Haines, Inc., Design #1703, 1964.

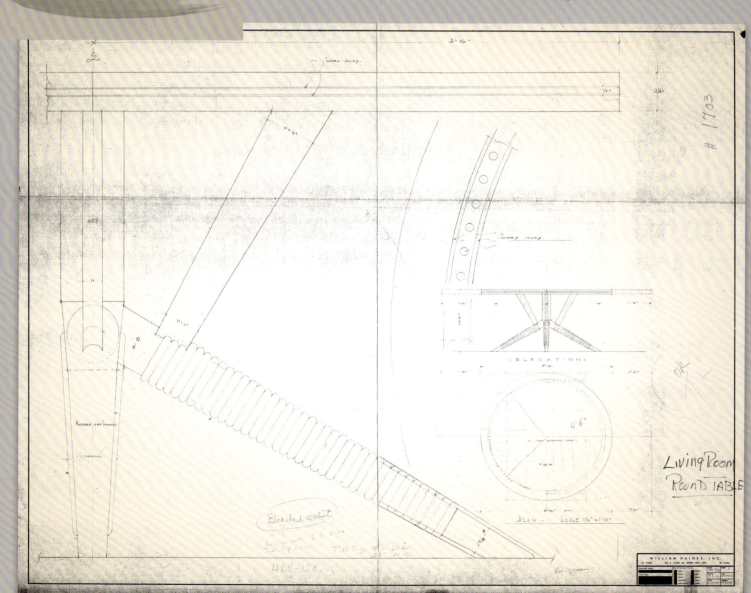

Finally, Haines smartly mirrors and pairs furnishings when there is room to do so. Entire setups of soft furnishings are duplicated and installed across from each other. There is never a single chair or side table. Its companion can be found juxtaposed or directly across from it. Pairs are found in chairs, sofas, chaise lounges, lamps, tabletop items, tables, and so on. This mathematical balance of furniture and accessories is critical to the soothing effect of his designs. As a result, spaces are organized and symmetrical.

Opposite
Sofa bench with Lucite and leather-wrapped coffee table with open trestle supports in primary bedroom. View of the sole cactus garden on the 200-acre property.

Below
Drawing of *Sofa Bench* with biscuit-tufting for primary bedroom. William Haines, Inc., Design #1692, 1964. A variation, *Window Bench* (without a backrest), was designed for Tom May in 1953 (William Haines, Inc., Design #679) but never executed. A note on the May drawing states "omit tufting."

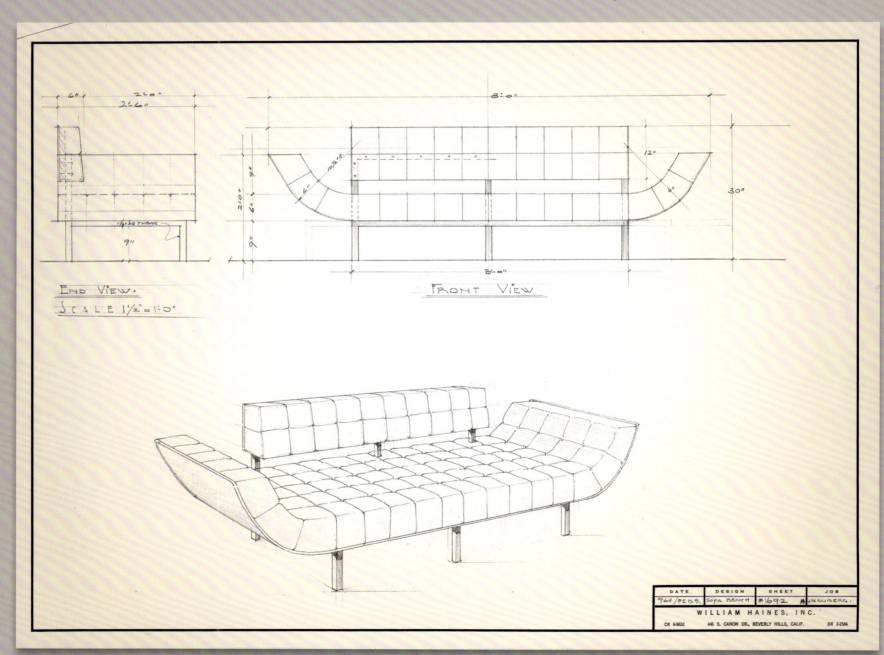

View of the Room of Memories featuring paneled walls, a skylight, dropped ceilings, and abundant integrated storage.

Integrated Art: Steuben Hallway

The Annenbergs' interest in cultural diplomacy—the intersection of art, culture, and international relations—took on a new significance in 1971. They commissioned from Steuben Glass a series of 36 crystal works, known as *Asian Artists in Crystal*. The offices at William Haines, Inc., requested that the pieces be delivered to them first so they could custom design the niches for a gallery to be built along the west side of the home. Architect Harry W. Saunders, AIA (1923–2013), was involved with the design work for the built-in display cases, which included six horizontal and three vertical wall openings covered in imported Italian blue-green silk velvet. The display case opening was set flush with the wall and finished in textured blue-green polished lacquer. A series of up-and-down lighting was installed to dramatically highlight each crystal piece as guests traveled through the Steuben hallway into the dining room.

Below
Walter Annenberg points out the *Asian Artists in Crystal* collection by Steuben Glass to Michael Deaver (left) and British Ambassador to the United State, Sir John Oliver Wright (right), in the Steuben hallway, 1982.

Opposite
Steuben Glass display case and console table in hallway.

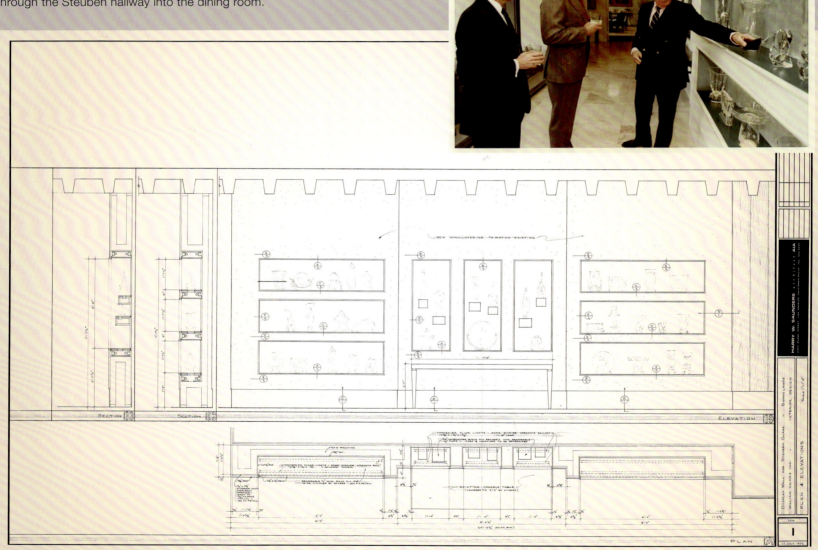

Above
Drawing of *Display Case for Steuben Glass*. Harry Saunders, Project #196 sheet 1, 1972.

Additional estate locations demonstrate Haines' site-specific designs tailored to a change in setting and usage intent. Each departs from the formality of the main house but remains in the overall vocabulary of the estate through the details. These include the Game Room with guest rooms and a variety of curated patio experiences adjacent to the main house.

Opposite

Red leather tub chairs with dark walnut frames for sunken bar area, and sunflower bouquet draperies. Haines was thoughtful about integrated storage, as seen here in tall cabinetry used for bar glasses and sunflower-motif dish sets.

Below

Yellow bamboo-style open armchair with leather seat detail.

Previous pages

Winter view of San Jacinto Mountains and landscape with mix-and-match suites of patio armchairs and lounges.

The Game Room Building

Exiting the house through a western-facing door, a short walk along a colonnade leads to a separate building that hosts the Game Room and two guest rooms. More game tables and a sunken bar await family and guests. Color imbues each of these spaces. Primary red and yellow dominate the Game Room, while the soft furnishings are in a nubby, friendly, heavy linen bursting with sunflower bouquets. Flanking the Game Room are two guest rooms that are mirrors of each other: the Yellow and Pink rooms. They are identical installations of bedroom furnishings and accessories along the color code. The fabrics include a lively, nubby linen stripe for the walls and draperies, while a feminine large-scale "scattered roses" motif in soft Swiss cotton covers the furnishings.

Above

Lucite boxes with netsuke figures fastened on lids are filled with jellybeans matching guest room colors.

Opposite

Sofa and ledge-back "Seniah" ("Haines" spelled backward) chair with hand-printed sunflower bouquet motif fabric.

Guest Wing

In 1977, some four years after William Haines died, the architect Harry Saunders was asked to design a guest wing, which housed three additional guest accommodations known as the Blue, Green, and Peach rooms. Ted Graber utilized the same design scheme and style as the two original guest rooms. This additional building was known as the guest extension, as it is integrated into the Game Room building via roof architecture, and provides a seamless design continuity to the overall appearance of this part of the estate.

Opposite

A richly glazed green lacquered table, bamboo-style open armchairs, and striped drapes work in concert to create an inviting corner in which to write letters while having a cup of tea in the Green Room.

Right

Green bamboo-style open armchair detail.

Outdoor Living

Sunnylands has expansive floor-to-ceiling glass walls that bring natural light inside the interiors as well as views of the lush grounds and distant western vistas of the San Jacinto Mountains. The concept of connecting outside and inside spaces is a core element of the desert living lifestyle. Patio and terrace areas are important parts of the Sunnylands setting and experience. Outdoor areas allow guests the opportunity to lounge, read, swim, enjoy a meal while admiring the scenic views, engage in the companionship of others, and relish in the hospitality of their hosts. Haines designed several outdoor casual and functional seating arrangements or "rooms without walls" to expand the living space, creating intimate and relaxing entertainment areas.

Above

Garden armchair with pierced circular openings and angular legs.

Opposite

Placing intricate tabletops under glass is a theme that continues from the indoor to the outdoor furnishings. Nesting tables are also a sub-theme that Haines incorporated in his designs.

Outdoor Furniture

The Sunnylands collection of over 100 pieces of patio and garden furniture was mostly designed by Haines with some sourced pieces. Original Haines designs may have found inspiration from wrought iron gates and fences that are stately, strong, and secure. The Klismos-style patio chairs and matching benches, designed with circles on the backrest, offer a midcentury streamlined appearance. Other design elements include crossbars, lattice, small circular punch-outs, floral flourishes, and tables with metal-ribbon-wrapped legs suggesting durability yet elegance. Patio and terrace furniture is fabricated in black iron frames with some painted in a verdigris texture finish. Glass or white marble is used for tabletops, and white vinyl cushions adorn chairs and lounges. A bench with angular legs appears like a hunched giant insect ready to pounce on prey and adds a unique, conversational piece to the patio area. The bench is part of a suite of outdoor furniture comprising pairs of chaise lounges, open armchairs, ottomans, and low tables.

Below
Drawing of *Breakfast Table* with laced arrow-shaped iron leg detail (see also pages 99, 101). William Haines, Inc., Design #1746, 1965.

Right
A patio chair with metal woven seat. The variety of outdoor furniture styles informs each space in a slightly different way, yet all work together.

Opposite
Regency-style garden bench with circular backrest.

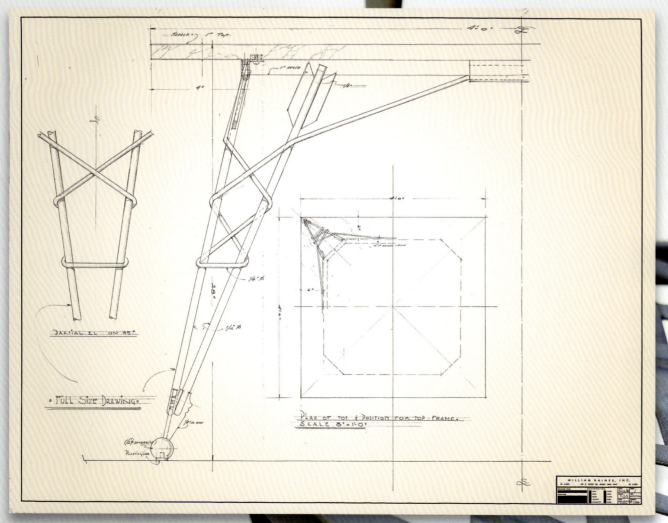

Integrated Art: Mosaic Tile Rugs

Walter and Haines began discussions in 1964 for an outdoor mosaic floor. Instead of purchasing an ancient mosaic floor, they settled upon the idea of interpreting antique fresco designs. Walter questioned the size of the mosaics to which Haines replied:

> We reviewed the sizes there with the furniture layout, and all of us agreed that the areas with the mosaics were in scale with the size of the garden and furniture.
>
> I feel if we cut down these areas we are going to lose the enormous impact of the mosaics, the original concept of which was to use them as rugs thrown in the garden.[14]

The William Haines, Inc., drawings, *Mosaic Floors Design for Living Terrace*, illustrate two outdoor mosaic tile "rugs" measuring 12'x28' and 12'x19'. The tiles set on the south terrace feature iconographies of flowering plants with birds and a central Medusa-like figure, while on the west patio, fruits and mammals with plants are displayed. These two define the key social spaces on the terrace.

Frugoli Marble Company executed the mosaics and E. B. Lohr and Company set the marble "rugs" in 1966. Patio chairs and tables sit atop the "rugs," creating additional outdoor dining areas for entertaining.

Above
Mosaic tile square depicting a Medusa-like figure detail, 1965.

Opposite
Breakfast table with arrow-shaped legs and marble top with Regency-style garden armchairs on mosaic tile "rug."

Above
Drawing of *Mosaic Floors Design for Living Terrace*. William Haines, Inc., Design #1745, 1965. Individual panels were manufactured in Italy with the design installed on the west terrace.

Foldout
Western view of the San Jacinto Mountains with patio furniture groupings and mosaic tile "rug."

DESIGN SIGNATURES

Color and Craftsmanship

Custom-crafted pieces are vital to the Haines design expression. His inspiration for the color choices at Sunnylands drew from nature—infinite blue and white cloudy desert skies, dramatic sunrises, and sunsets of pink, yellow, orange, and violet, along with the green and tan landscapes.

Haines hired craftspeople, workshops, and local artisans to execute his designs and in 1963 was one of the few decorators offering full design services. "Haines was like a film director, thoughtfully composing furniture and interiors, supervising various people while allowing for creativity (and credit) to help produce his vision for each client" noted one architectural scholar.[15] Haines utilized a variety of surface finishes, color treatments, wood choices, and upholstery styles to provide high-end distinctiveness to his furniture and room designs. The craftspeople he hired to carry out his commissions made the highest quality furniture and provided each client with an elevated level of sophistication and exclusivity.

Previous pages

Backgammon table and conference chairs with walnut paneled back and turquoise leather seat, and a pair of Qing Dynasty pottery dogs on dark pedestal base, armature table lamp in the Royal Sitting Room. The Annenbergs reportedly played backgammon at this table each evening when guests were not in residence.

Right

A variety of wood board samples featuring color treatments, finishes, lacquers, and varnishes for use at Sunnylands, circa 1964–1965.

Opposite

Detail of green painted table and Lucite box with netsuke figure fastened on lid and green jellybeans. The concept of Hollywood Regency design is inherent in the design of this Haines box. The modern material Lucite represents "Hollywood," while the antique ivory netsuke figure, an Asian element, represents "Regency."

Custom-made

Decorative and custom-made pieces play a critical role in the Haines design canon. Based on a client project inventory, the firm created over 100 design drawings and sketches for the Annenbergs from 1964 to 1977. These include room and furniture layout plans as well as drawings for cabinets, tables, consoles, sofas, desks, chairs, trapunto quilting, shelving, and more. The custom furniture for Sunnylands was manufactured by the fine craftspeople of Los Angeles businesses such as Prentice Company, Howard Robin, and others. More than 450 pieces of original custom-made items make Sunnylands the largest extant collection of Haines' designs produced specifically for a residence as it was intended and as it was lived in.

Opposite

Detail of backgammon table with open legs and secret drawer to stow away game pieces, and conference chair in turquoise leather and walnut.

Below

Drawing of *Game Table* for backgammon. Williams Haines, Inc., Design #1705, 1964.

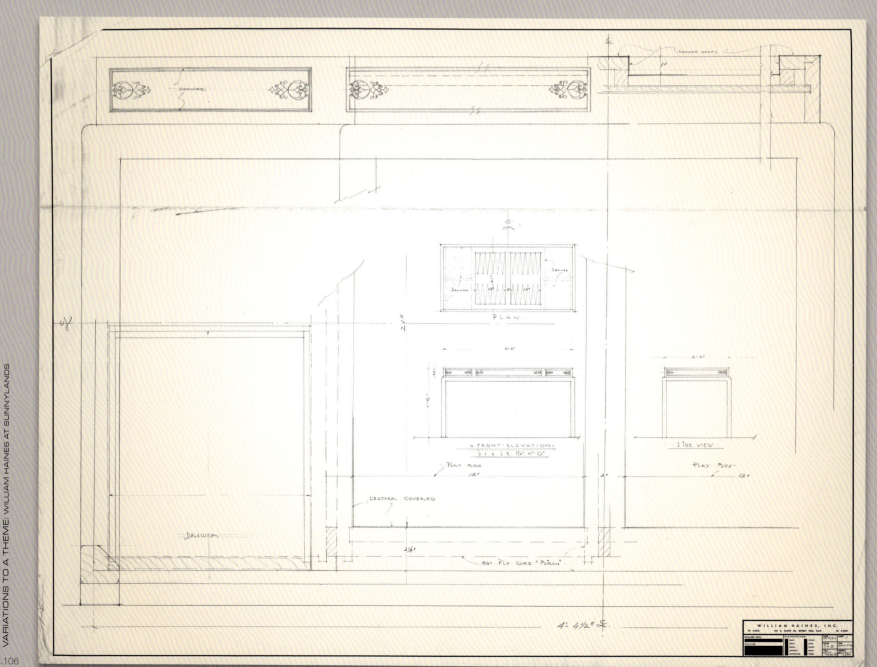

Texture

In the art world, seven visual elements are considered the main avenues of communication through an object: space, form, line, shape, color, value of color hue, and texture. Considering furniture as a work of art, these elements are applicable.

Used adeptly, texture informs an object in myriad ways via perception and, in the case of furniture, also through tactile experience. In Haines' playbook, texture is both real (quilted fabrics providing a luxurious physical and visual experience) and imagined (faux stone, tortoiseshell, and brick-motif). Guests to Sunnylands occasionally inquire whether Haines' heavily glazed tables evoking malachite are in fact made of real stone. His choice of textures challenges our perception of materiality, enlisting a variety of dyed leathers, Thai silks, nubby linens, colorful tile mosaics, and more. Haines was a master at layering real and imagined textures in one tableau.

Opposite

Button-tufted yellow silk fabric bench with open trestle supports and Lucite top lamp table with antique carved wood eagle-form on rock outcropping, one of a pair and believed to be the only pair ever executed. The eagle likely references the Annenbergs' American patriotism.

Below

Drawing of *Lamp Table (Eagle)* with Lucite top and carved wood base. William Haines, Inc., Design #1713, 1964.

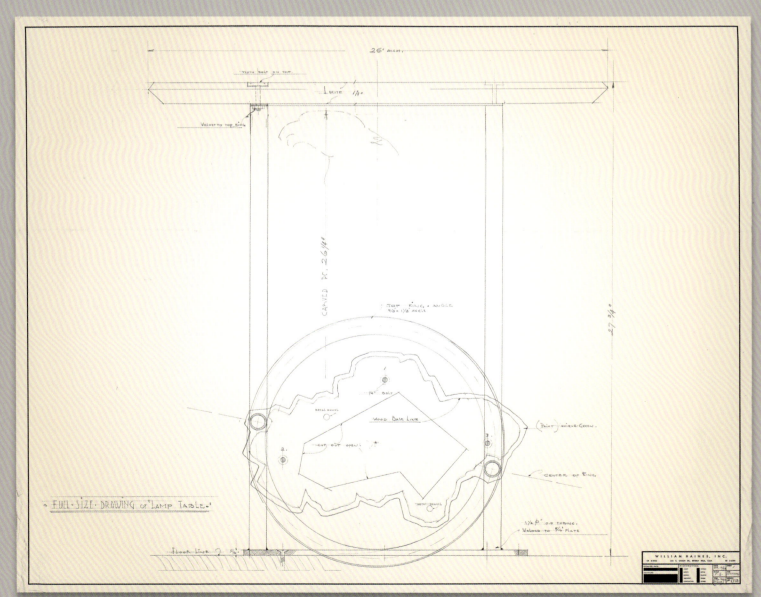

Shape

If one has ever sat on an uncomfortable chair, one knows how important shape, including line and contoured form, is to furniture design. Ergonomic geometry reigns supreme in furniture design. Haines' furniture is known for its handsome volumes, bold intersections of various planes, and sexy angularity while miraculously remaining approachable and achieving "sink-into-it" comfort. Prolonged meals are encouraged by the luxurious shape and feel of the dining chairs, and cocktail conversations aspire to be never-ending when one is settled into a Haines sofa.

Right
The original Brentwood Chair (popular name: Hostess Chair) is "versatile, modern, and luxurious," according to the firm William Haines Designs, which continues to make a version of the chair. Executed in gray leather for the living room, this is one of six that surround a hexagonal *gemütlich* [cozy] table.

Opposite
Detail of oak-stained tub-back caned chair with black leather seat and square flared legs. One of a pair by Graber for the Game Room.

Juxtaposition

Haines is known for paired lamps, but he also juxtaposed entire suites of furniture across from their mirror images. Haines was celebrated for his deep understanding of art history and boldly mixing pieces across historic periods. In pairing figurative works, including Auguste Rodin's life-size depiction of *Eve* (1881) with Tang Dynasty-era funerary figures (618–906 AD), he cleverly interweaves 1,000 years of disparate art history in a glance, providing a stimulating visual experience.

Opposite

Tang Dynasty glazed pottery figures of a camel and Lokapala (tomb guardian) are juxtaposed with a modern bronze masterpiece sculpture by Auguste Rodin, *Eve*, spanning 1,000 years of figurative art.

Below

Annenberg residence proposed addendum for furnishings and cost estimate from William Haines, Inc., July 1, 1964. The Annenbergs were natural archivists and retained their records, providing a fascinating study of Haines' process.

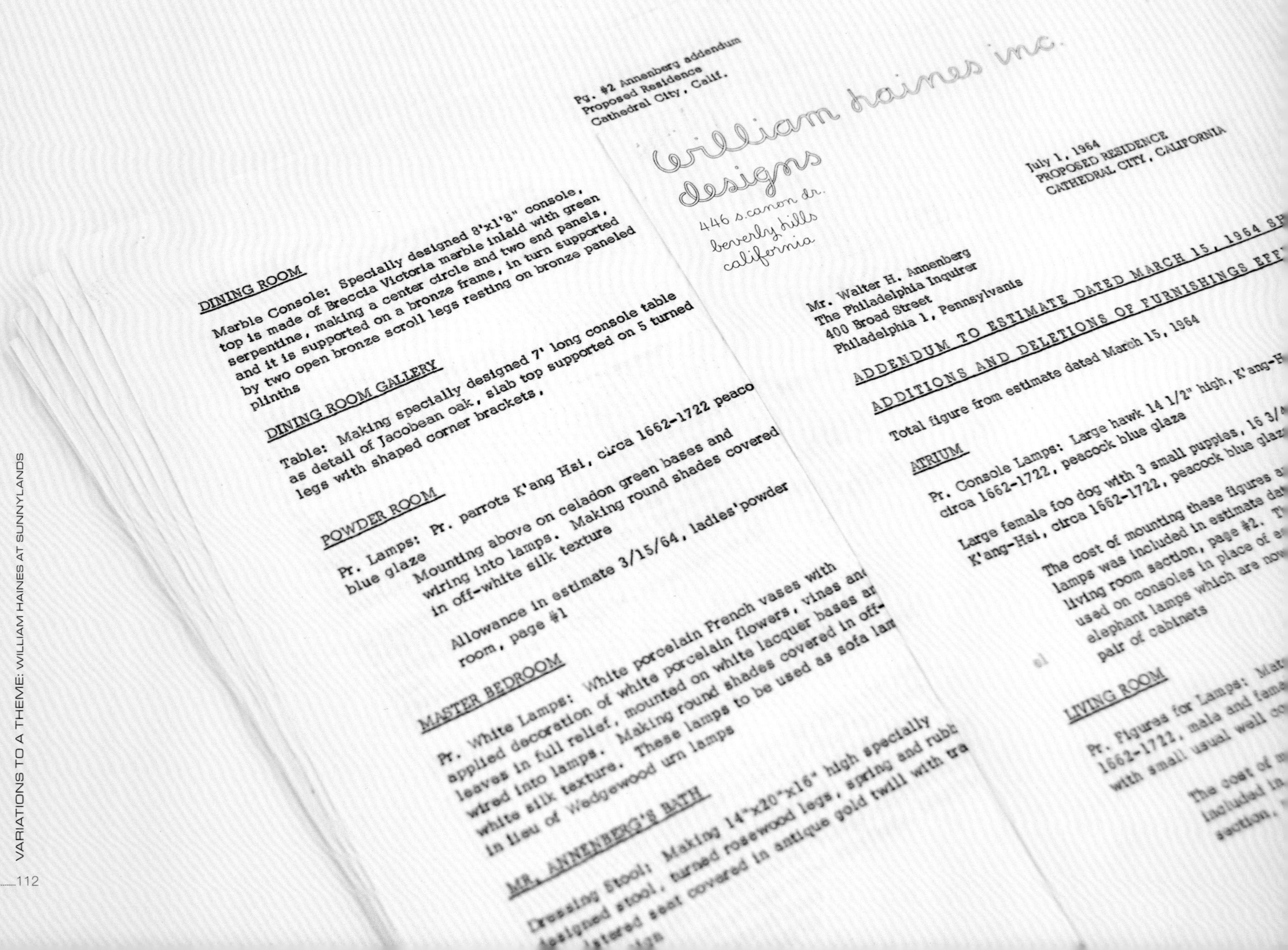

Composition

Easier said than done: successful interior composition—the arrangement of multiple items—results in a balanced space, delivering a pleasing, visceral sense of overall order. Feng shui enthusiasts suggest that the calm one feels in a well-designed space is, principally, because of thoughtful, cohesive design. Well-composed furniture plans signal how to enter the space, where to place a handbag or briefcase, whether the scene is stiff or casual, where to sit, where to stand, and where to set drinks. A welcoming layout of furniture might offer each seated guest a triangle of two people to talk to, be supplemented by flattering lighting, and result in calming every nerve for first-time guests. Few can challenge Haines' mastery of composition.

Right
Peach Room furniture and accessory composition illustrates the pleasing impact of thoughtful design.

Opposite
One of six seating arrangement compositions in the living room provides an intimate setup for two in which to relax surrounded by beauty.

Scale

Those who have experienced the truism that everything is relative will inherently understand that scale is one of the most crucial considerations when creating a furniture plan for a space. In the same square footage, the scale of the furnishings and architecture dictates whether the space feels large, overwhelming, alienating, crowded, too small for the furniture—or ideally just right. The raised pyramidal ceiling height experienced upon entry at Sunnylands signals that this is a palatial space. Did Haines lean into filling the space with one enormously scaled, James Bondian, contiguous, circular sofa seating 25? No, and predictably, given his experience creating scenes that make people both feel and look good, he utilized scale to create a series of welcoming, comfortable, and attractive areas in a large expanse.

Opposite

One of five seating arrangement compositions in the Atrium. Jean Arp's bronze sculpture *Déméter*, 1960, is framed in the window atop an Arp-designed wood pedestal.

Below

Haines' annotations in red pencil for the *Plan of Living Room Area*. A. Quincy Jones and Frederick E. Emmons, Project #246 sheet, 1964.

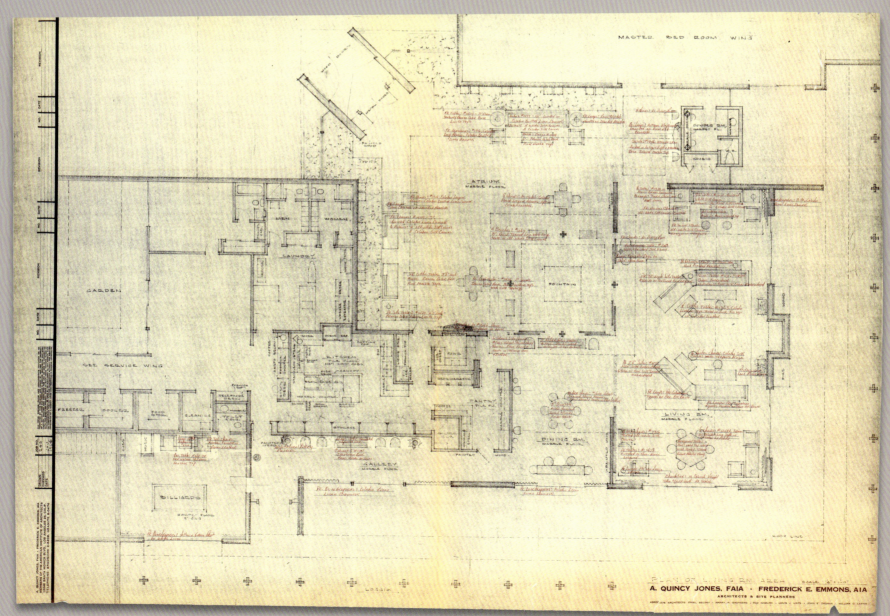

Trapunto

Even the most jaded furniture experts marvel at the collection of soft furnishings festooned with trapunto quilting at Sunnylands. Trapunto, an art form nearly extinct today, is the process of hand-quilting designs in raised relief tailored to each fabric panel of the furnishing (for instance, one scene in relief on the seat of a chair and another on the back of the chair). The overall effect is breathtaking. Haines designed trapunto treatments for the primary sofa groupings, including chairs and pull-up hostess stools, in three seating areas at Sunnylands. Raising the luxury bar yet another level, Haines designed crewel embroidered flowers to lay atop trapunto quilting, resembling a garden trellis, on the six central soft furnishings in the living room.

Opposite

Diamond-shaped, trapunto-quilted sofa, upholstered circular hostess stools, and gold tooling embellishments on leather-wrapped coffee table provided, and continue to provide, the perfect setting for presidents, prime ministers, and leaders across various fields today.

Below

Drawing of *Stool Upholstering Design* for trapunto-quilting. William Haines, Inc., Design #1720, circa 1964-1965 (see also cover and pages 2-3, 67, 119). Haines designed low circular hostess stools with various upholstery treatments, solid colors, and some even with swivels. These were easily tucked under coffee tables for the purpose of providing additional seating.

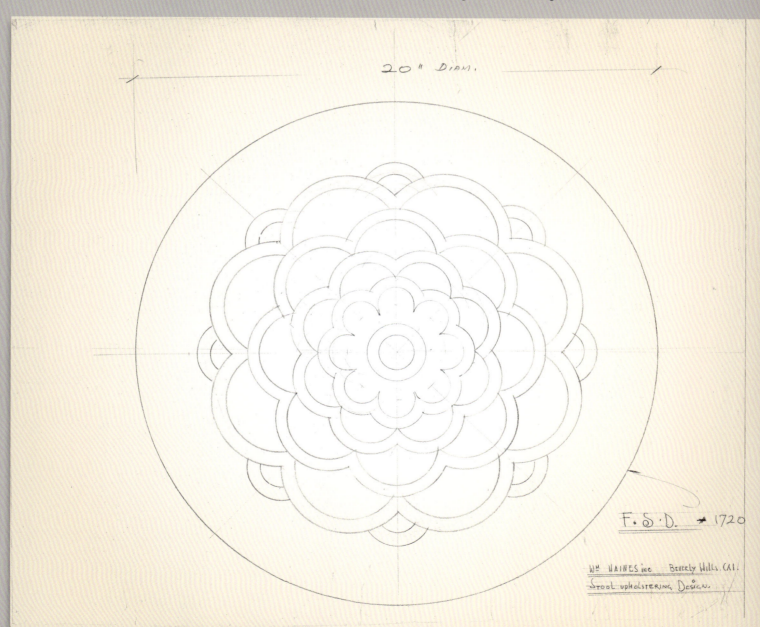

Tufting

Leaving no fabric behind for special treatments, Haines' vocabulary included the modern version of tufting. At Sunnylands, he executed a variety of tufting designs but none more than a "biscuit" layout, known for the resulting shape that resembles a batch of the bread product, biscuit. Haines often tufted already-textured fabrics, creating layered dimensionality. Both elegant and inviting, his buttoned tufting technique creates an alluring three-dimensional landscape to enjoy.

Right

Drawing of *Bench* with biscuit-tufting detail (see also page 109). William Haines, Inc., Design #1718, 1964.

Opposite

Biscuit-tufting on sofa bench with textured weave fabric in raised relief.

Foldout

The view from the living room toward the front entrance illustrates the importance of flowers and plants in the design, both real and imagined, and exemplifies bringing the outside inside the house.

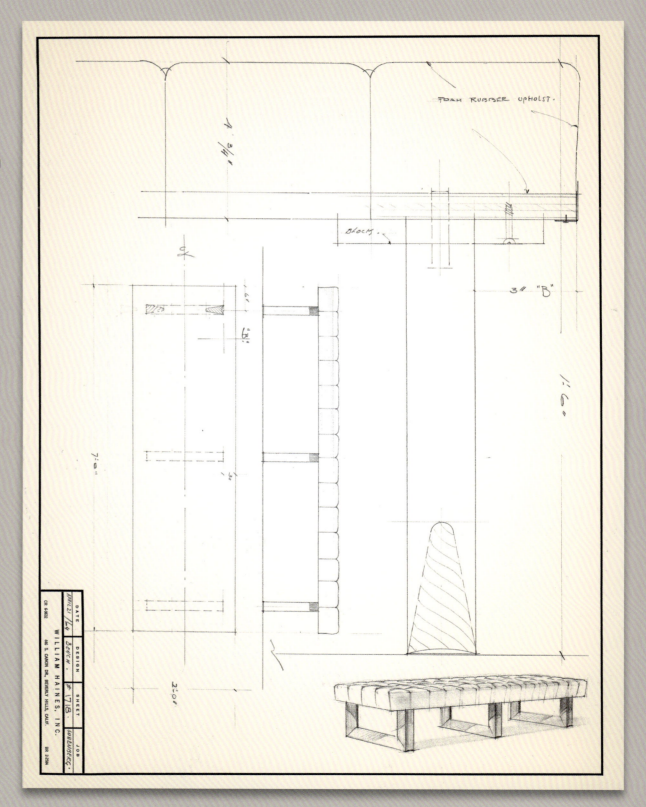

Inlay

Haines was self-taught, and his path toward interior design work began with antique dealing. He was arguably encyclopedic on material culture across design eras, and so antique furniture inlays inevitably caught his eye. Because each piece of furniture in his design plans was custom-made for clients, each piece provided a new stylistic adventure. Table edges are an area of focus for Haines on which to add high-end interest. Exotic woods, shell, and ivory inlays delight the eye throughout the furniture collection amid a variety of other treatments, such as stamped gold tooling embellishments that adorns many leather chairs and tabletops. The result is furniture that achieves elevated luxury, given its inlays and other decorative elements, while the inherent design lines pull the furniture back toward being modern in appearance.

Below

Detail: Brazilian rosewood pedestal dining table inlaid with ivory-beaded band on an outer walnut-banded design. One of two dining tables of graduated sizes each with two leaves.

Opposite

Detail: Hexagon-shaped table made of a variety of woods with canted edge and inlays of ivory and flower bandings. Haines used the German word *gemütlich* [cozy] to convey that he envisioned this table to be built specifically for relaxing with others; its height is intentionally lower than that of a dining table.

Lighting

Room lighting is an essential design element in creating a comfortable space. Haines was a master at creating one-of-a-kind table and floor lamps for his clients. His armature custom lamps not only serve the essential function of lighting but also bring into play a vital design component by adding ambiance and personality to a room. At Sunnylands, objets d'art were transformed into lamps either in pairs or with two identical objects on a single base surmounted by a suitably shaped lampshade. The use of chinoiserie porcelain, vases, figurines, and sculptures—primarily flora and fauna themes—are signature trademarks in a Haines lamp. Great care was taken not to drill into the item so as not to lessen its value, but rather, an armature was built around the object to support it as a lamp. The object is thus preserved and becomes a self-illuminating lamp. Chinese ceramics and animals such as oxen, Foo dogs, parrots, lions, and elephants are found as lamps at Sunnylands. A Haines lamp offers whimsy as well as a visual interest:

> Billy Haines lamps are design legend. The Annenbergs' collection of subtly colored Tang Dynasty pottery and vivid Chinese cloisonné enamels played nicely with the French art. Wonderful works of art were mounted on tall bases or even low columns and were lit with taut, silk drum lampshades. The lamps are dramatic and elegant, providing beautiful illumination for the artifacts.[16]

Opposite

A pair of spectacular yellow porcelain vases molded with the "Hundred Antiques" motif, a compilation of a scholar's interests. Mounted as lamps for the primary bedroom, these flank a one-of-a-kind, button-tufted sofa bench with the seat continuing up into armrests.

Left

Though Haines demonstrated a strong predilection for Chinese objects as subjects for lamps, including this polychrome terracotta figure (near left), Graber often included Japanese objects in his curation of lamps, including this bronze figure of a man riding an ox (far left).

In the living room hangs a modern chandelier made of wrought iron, brass, and gold leaf, designed by Haines himself. The 16-branch candle bulbs are supported by a cylindrical stem and two graduated tiers with spiral-twist and scroll arms. The Annenbergs would repurpose many of their own lamps from various properties and send them to Haines for repairs, rework, or new shades. The Sunnylands Collections and Exhibition staff has cataloged 72 table lamps, including 22 pairs found on the estate, with more in storage yet to be inventoried.

In a letter dated May 18, 1964, to Leonore, Haines writes of his excitement at finding a pair of jars to be made as lamps:

I was most fortunate at buying in the south some superb pieces for lamps: a great pair of white porcelain de Paris vases incrusted with the most delicate three-dimensional white flowers for your bedroom.

I have Ch'ien Lung parrots, the most elegant Chinese hawk—all in that blue-green for the living room. I am going to take the elephants out of the atrium (find a substitution) and use them in the living room with the foregoing birds, and they, together with the dogs, will make the most amazing arrangement of lamps for the center of the room. They are the proper quality.[17]

Right

Detail: A spectacular Meissen-style white glazed baluster jar, mounted as a table lamp (likely Samson) with applied relief of floral branches, resides in the Peach Room, one of a pair.

Opposite

Chandelier with 16-branch arms, in wrought iron with embellishments of gold leaf, hangs from the coffered ceiling. While not immediately apparent as a Haines design, the metalwork is echoed in the Haines table installed below the chandelier.

In reviewing the early decorating service proposal and invoices, two extensive lamp description entries for July 1, 1964, stand out:

Master Bedroom—Pair white porcelain French vases with applied decoration of white porcelain flowers, vines, and leaves in full relief, mounted white lacquer bases and wired into lamps. Making round shades covered in off-white silk texture. These lamps are to be used as sofa lamps in lieu of Wedgewood urn lamps.

Blue Room—Pair of square Chinese vases, turquoise background with birds and water lilies decoration mounted on top and bottom members finished in turquoise lacquer and wired into lamps. Making round shades covered in white textured linen.[18]

Right

One of a pair of Chinese, turquoise-glazed models of birds, mounted as lamps. This expressive figure occupies the vanity in the ladies' powder room off the living room.

Opposite

One of a pair of oxen, this Chinese, mustard-glazed figure, originally a roof tile and mounted as a lamp using Lucite and a walnut base, lights the way in the Room of Memories hallway.

Below

Haines' remarkable renderings depict exact groupings of furniture, lighting, and accessories envisioned for each space.

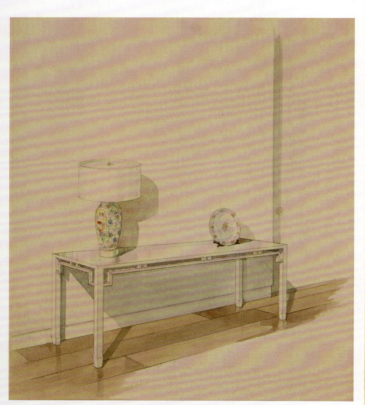

Pillows

Haines used down-filled silk throw pillows on his sofas, chairs, and beds, mainly in a 16- or 20-square-inch solid color. Lumbar pillows with matching fabrics on the diamond-shaped quilted couches and chairs are bountiful. For Walter's 70th birthday in 1978, a monogrammed needlepoint cushion with the initials "WA" was a gift from Ted Graber, who designed and made the pillow. A similar pillow with the initials "RR" was a gift to President Ronald Reagan on his 70th birthday in 1981 from Graber.

Walter wrote about his gift pillow on March 13, 1978:

Dear Ted,

The pillow for my Room of Memories underscores the quality and character of all the things you do. It might even be at the expense of another job as you indicated the other night which, of course, gave me a great chuckle—but the remark did have a touch of class.

Sincerely,

Walter Annenberg[19]

Opposite

"WA" needlepoint pillow, a gift from Ted Graber on Walter Annenberg's 70th birthday.

Below

Letter from Walter to Graber regarding needlepoint pillow gift, March 13, 1978.

Below

"WA" pillow rests between Secretary of State Alexander Haig and President Ronald Reagan in conversation in the Room of Memories, 1982.

Perhaps included in the same gift was a suite of five petit-point down-filled pillows of beige, coral, and white yarns. In the primary bedroom, a favorite pillow with multiple Sunnylands sun emblems rests on the custom sofa bench with biscuit tufting. Several pillows in the house were gifts to the Annenbergs rather than original Haines or Graber selections. The Annenbergs particularly treasured and enjoyed pillows with clever and witty sayings that added to the relaxed warmth and humor of a room.

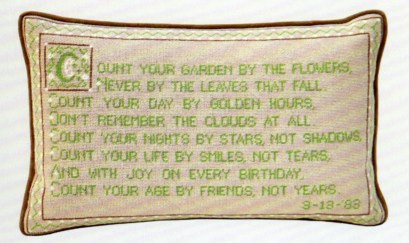

This page

Decorative pillows with phrases and quotes are a popular feature in the guest rooms. According to the Annenbergs' former estate manager, Michael Comerford, these pillows were either handmade gifts or sourced by Graber.

Opposite

Pillow with multiple Sunnylands sun emblems rests on the sofa bench in the primary bedroom.

Bibelots

Another Haines design feature is the use of small, decorative objects or trinkets placed atop tables and other surfaces. As is evident from a review of a number of his project invoices, Haines selected and procured a large assortment of bibelot items, such as Lucite cigarette boxes, animal figurines, porcelain Chinese and Japanese plates, cups, vases, bowls, fabric-covered matchboxes, flower holders, wastebaskets, and other curios. Leonore displayed her gifts, mementos, small enamel boxes, and other keepsakes on surface areas as well. Additionally, in keeping with the Hollywood Regency style of displaying attractive objects of interest, tabletop items also include modern sculpture by Jean Arp and Émile Gilioli, important carved Chinese jade and jadeite boulders, and best-in-class cloisonné metalworks. Curiosities on the cabinets and tables hail from Italy, France, England, and Denmark. Luxury makers such as Steuben Glass, Boucheron, Buccellati, Georg Jensen, Tiffany & Co., and Cartier provide ample joy for the eyes.

Right
Drawing of *Desk Master Bedroom* with single-turned tapered leg. William Haines, Inc., Design #1752, 1965.

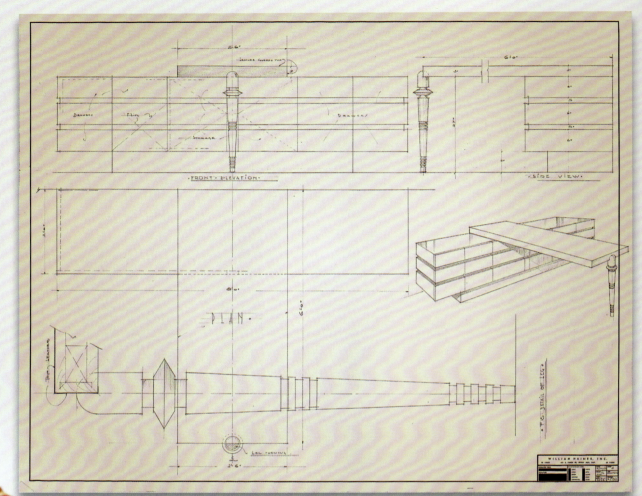

Opposite
Leonore's cantilevered writing table with leather-wrapped top and single-turned tapered leg coupled with a 12-drawer credenza. A pair of ceramic glazed parrots mounted as a desk lamp stand below floating wall shelves with Chinese and English porcelain items in primary bedroom.

Left
Assortment of tabletop bibelots from around the world, from left to right: archaic bronze wine vessel, Shang Dynasty; French porcelain Samson double fish vase; Japanese Kutani porcelain box and cover; Chinese famille verte porcelain jug, Kangxi Period; Pre-Columbian terracotta vessel on tripod stand.

Integrated Art: Paintings

The wondrous assembly of tabletop confections serves as a complement to the primary focus of the Annenbergs' art collecting: their world-famous Impressionist and Post-Impressionist painting collection, now on permanent display at the Metropolitan Museum of Art (Met) in New York City. These famous paintings, now known as The Annenberg Collection, migrated in the 1970s to adorn every wall in the tent at Sunnylands. As the collection grew and Sunnylands became the Annenbergs' primary hub for entertaining over the years, the couple had the paintings permanently installed at Sunnylands rather than at their once-main residence near Philadelphia.

Haines and Graber, along with the Annenbergs, reportedly carried the paintings about, and through trial and error, curated their final placement. Today, Met-produced replicas inform the spaces where the originals were once placed, reminding viewers of how central they are to the collecting interest of the Annenbergs and their home.

The Annenbergs bequeathed their 53 paintings to the Met in 1991. At the time, Walter stated: "I think that ultimately, fine art should belong to the public, not to any one individual."[20]

Below

The *New York Times* front page announcing the gift to the Metropolitan Museum of Art (Met) in New York City of The Annenberg Collection of Impressionist and Post-Impressionist paintings, March 12, 1991. The collection was transferred to the Met in 2002.

Opposite

Since 2002, full-scale replicas of the famed Annenberg Collection of Impressionist and Post-Impressionist paintings have hung on the walls at Sunnylands, providing a permanent record of their final residential placement.

A DESIGN LEGACY PRESERVED

Haines held firm to a strict adherence to avoid cliché designs. It is a testament to William Haines and to Ted Graber that these intact interiors remain as timeless and glorious today as they were in 1966. Many consider Sunnylands the apex of Haines' design achievements, along with another Annenberg project, Winfield House (the U.S. Ambassador's residence) in London. The interior design for Sunnylands was the most prestigious commission among the firm's illustrious, celebrated, and long-lasting achievements. Under a Mayan-inspired pyramidal roof, it was able to successfully achieve an integrated, timeless, and graceful living space based on the attuned vision of its loyal clients Leonore and Walter Annenberg. Haines wrote to the couple on May 19, 1964, regarding his design aesthetic, and stated: "It occurred to me that there are variations to a theme,"[21] which could appropriately be the motto for this extraordinary 20th-century design firm.

Previous pages
The level of handcrafted detail and hours of fabrication involved in Haines' furniture has been compared to that of a couture gown. This is demonstrated here in a dining table's four mahogany flared supports on ring-turned, splayed legs. A kinetic, bronze sculpture is seen in the courtyard, *Peacock*, 1961, by Harry Bertoia.

Opposite
Walnut and red leather-wrapped library table with gold tooling embellishments, trestle supports and nested low table, one of a pair in the Room of Memories. Haines cleverly tucked away extra chairs, stools, and in this case an extra table, anticipating every possible need of his clients.

Below
Leonore and Walter Annenberg enjoy a happy moment in their living room, 1983.

Opposite

Console with pink marble top and C-scroll supports is integrated into the wall and provides a surface to display rare china in the dining room.

Below

Drawing of *Detail of Bronze Console* with marble top. William Haines, Inc., Design #1731, 1964.

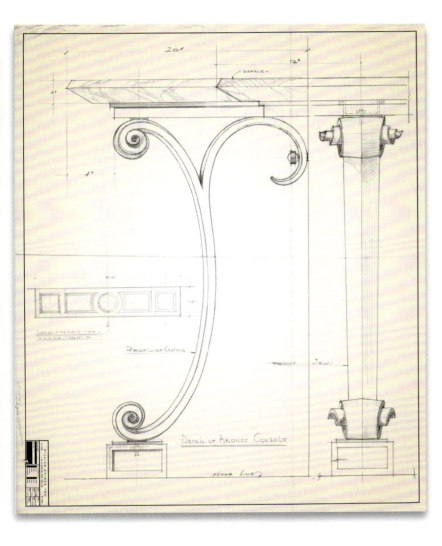

Endnotes

1. Rus, Mayer, "Strange Alchemy: A. Quincy Jones and William Haines," in *A. Quincy Jones: Building for Better Living*, edited by Brooke Hodge (Los Angeles and Munich: Hammer Museum and DelMonico Books, 2013), 126.
2. Head, Jeffrey, "William Haines" in *Modern Americana: Studio Furniture from High Craft to High Glam*, edited by Todd Merrill and Julie V. Iovine (New York: Rizzoli, 2008), 248.
3. Memory, Mary, "Design Dialogues: The World of Ted Graber," *Architectural Digest*, 38: (7), July 1981, 166.
4. Haines, William, "Designer William Haines' Outspoken Comments," *Architectural Digest*, 29: (2) September/October 1972, 13.
5. Ibid.
6. Postcard transcript from Walter Annenberg to William Haines, December 14, 1964, Sunnylands Collection, Rancho Mirage, California, 2009.1.3932.
7. Letter from William Haines to Walter Annenberg, February 23, 1965, Sunnylands Collection, Rancho Mirage, California, 2009.1.3932.
8. Sunnylands Guest Book 1: 1966 to 1984, Sunnylands Collection, Rancho Mirage, California, 2009.1.3252.
9. Radcliffe, Donnie, "For Leonore Annenberg, It's Lovely at the Top," *The Washington Post*, July 12, 1981, https://www.washingtonpost.com/archive/lifestyle/1981/07/12/for-leonore-annenberg-its-lovely-at-the-top/b8c104d0-9cdc-4b72-b99a-9cd0f8606745/ Accessed October 18, 2022.
10. Lockwood, Charles, "Tour Jack L. Warner's House in Beverly Hills," *Architectural Digest*, April 1992, https://www.architecturaldigest.com/story/jack-l-warner-beverly-hills-house. Accessed October 18, 2022.
11. Ibid.
12. Letter from Walter Annenberg to Franc Shor, October 4, 1963, Sunnylands Collection, Rancho Mirage, California, 2009.1.3930.
13. Frauchiger, Fritz, "Annenberg's Sunnylands," *Rancho Mirage Playground of the Presidents*, 1991, 32.
14. Letter from William Haines to Walter Annenberg, May 25, 1965, Sunnylands Collection, Rancho Mirage, California, 2009.1.3932.
15. Head, op. cit., 243.
16. Maloney, Carey, "The Talented Mr. Haines: Onetime actor Billy Haines rose to become one of the biggest stars in Hollywood … it just wasn't in front of a camera," *Palm Springs Life*, September 1, 2005, https://www.palmspringslife.com/the-talented-mr-haines/ Accessed June 8, 2022.
17. Letter from William Haines to Leonore Annenberg, May 18, 1964, Sunnylands Collection, Rancho Mirage California, 2009.1.3931.
18. Invoices from Williams Haines, Inc., to Walter Annenberg, July 1, 1964. Sunnylands Collection, Rancho Mirage, California, 2009.1.3931.
19. Letter from Walter Annenberg to Ted Graber, March 13, 1978, Sunnylands Collection, Rancho Mirage, California, 2009.1.3929.
20. Horowitz, Craig, "The Respectable Mr. Annenberg," *M: The Civilized Man*, April 1984, 67.
21. Letter from William Haines to Walter and Leonore Annenberg, May 19, 1964, Sunnylands Collection, Rancho Mirage, California, 2009.1.3931.

Additional Resources

De Long, David G. (editor), *Sunnylands: Art and Architecture of the Annenberg Estate in Rancho Mirage, California* (Philadelphia: University of Pennsylvania Press, 2009).

Lyle, Janice, *Sunnylands: America's Midcentury Masterpiece*. Exp. and Rev. ed. (New York: The Vendome Press, 2016).

Mann, William J., *Wisecracker: The Life and Times of William Haines, Hollywood's First Openly Gay Star* (New York: Penguin Books, 1998).

Schifando, Peter, and Jean H. Mathison, *Class Act: William Haines Legendary Hollywood Decorator* (New York: Pointed Leaf Press, 2005).

Opposite

Hand-painted, faux wood grain paneling adorns a wall in the primary bedroom. The lamp is one of a pair of famille rose, coral-ground porcelain vases mounted as a lamp, circa 1965. As with many of Haines' lamps, this lamp is integrated into the furniture, so cords are out of sight.

Acknowledgments

The famous Austrian architect Harry Seidler once said, "Good design doesn't date." The timelessness of Sunnylands' architecture, landscape, interior design, and furniture collection provides a superb illustrated example of this claim. The interiors for Sunnylands were one of William Haines' final acts and arguably amount to his most celebrated design today.

We thank the following people for contributing to the exhibition, this catalog, and accompanying programs in celebration of the incomparable William Haines at Sunnylands. The Board of Trustees of The Annenberg Foundation Trust at Sunnylands provided generous support for the exhibition and this publication. Trustees are Wallis Annenberg, Lauren Bon, Diane Deshong, Howard Deshong III, Leonore Deshong, Elizabeth Kabler, Elizabeth Sorensen, Charles Annenberg Weingarten, and Gregory Annenberg Weingarten. David J. Lane, president of The Annenberg Foundation Trust at Sunnylands, and Mike Ellzey, chief of estate and operations, also provided invaluable support.

Patrick Dragonette, a well-known authority on Haines, contributed his insights to this catalog and furnished historical context to the Haines story at Sunnylands. Historic fabric experts Julie Kaminska and Bob Bitter of Fret Fabrics supported editorially on matters of fabric composition and treatments. Greg Bianchini, Lucile Lac, and Peter Schifando of William Haines Designs shared archives and paint and glaze sample boards as well as their knowledge of the techniques Haines and his artisans enlisted to create each custom piece.

Sunnylands' archivist and librarian, Frank Lopez, and I co-wrote this catalog and co-curated the exhibition. Frank's meticulous research elevated our understanding of Haines at Sunnylands. The collections and exhibitions department staff supported and executed the catalog and exhibition. They are Mary Velez, Noah Johns, and consultant to the archives Michael Comerford, who provided his memories of Haines himself participating in the curation of painting placements, among other recollections.

Additional Sunnylands staff who helped with the project were Ashley Santana, editor, who ensured the quality of the catalog text and layout. Mike Reeske, David Montoya, Gerardo DeLeon, and the entire facilities team prepared the exhibition space. Ken Chavez and Eric Ornelas of the communications department added their expertise in marketing the exhibition. Michaeleen Gallagher and the education staff—Ivonne Miranda Correa and Vanessa Smith—supported the exhibition through innovative programming.

Additional people outside Sunnylands were instrumental in a variety of ways. Kamil Beski of Beski Projekts led the fabrication and installation of the exhibition. Lighting designer Geoff Korf illuminated the exhibition beautifully. Mark Woodworth provided stellar editorial services. Finally, the celebrated photographer David Loftus created insightful photographs for this catalog, which was expertly designed and art-directed by John Crummay and Robin Rout of JCRR Design.

Anne Rowe
Director of Heritage

The Annenberg Foundation Trust at Sunnylands acknowledges the people who first lived in the Coachella Valley and whose descendants reside here today. Sunnylands occupies a space where indigenous people gathered and built community. We hope that engaging in important conversations on national and world affairs honors those who came before us.

Overleaf

Japanese bronze crane-figure table lamp seen through green bamboo-style open armchair back.